Einstein's Science Parties

EASY PARTIES FOR CURIOUS KIDS

Shar Levine and Allison Grafton

John Wiley & Sons
New York • Chichester • Brisbane • Toronto • Singapore

In memory of Max Levine, my father and my friend.
And, as always, to my husband, Paul, my children, Shira and Josh, and my mother, Dorothy. Thanks for everything, especially the new computer.

—S.L.

To Shar and Terry for their hard work and creative minds. And to all the children in Einstein's science classes and birthday parties, without whose participation this book would not have been possible.

—A.G.

Our thanks to the children and parents who over the last five years have had parties from Einstein's. We have enjoyed it as much as you have. To Henning Hald at Ocean Coast Dry Ice, our everlasting gratitude for your technical advice, and to Maurice Bridge, who finds the files when they're lost, thanks.

Library of Congress Cataloging-in-Publication Data

Levine, Shar, 1953-
    Einstein's science parties: easy parties for curious kids/Shar Levine and
Allison Grafton.
        p. cm.
        Includes index.
        ISBN 0-471-59646-9
        1. Scientific recreations—Juvenile literature. 2. Science—Experiments—Juvenile literature. 3. Children's parties—Juvenile literature. [1. Scientific recreations. 2. Science—Experiments. 3. Experiments. 4. Parties.] I. Grafton, Allison. II. Title.
Q164.L47 1994
793.2'1—dc20   93-33107

Printed in the United States of America
10 9 8 7 6 5 4 3 2 1

Contents

Introduction

Children's parties used to be simple things! The party was thrown in the child's home. There would be food, usually sandwiches, or hot dogs and chips. The drinks, made from sugary powdered mixes, were served in plastic cups. The cake was homemade and decorated with icing and candy. Kids played games and made their own fun.

In the '90s, kids' parties have evolved and seem to have taken on a life of their own. Today, birthdays have become productions requiring entertainers, restaurant meals, alternative party settings, fancy cakes, and expensive goodie bags. A parent can spend $10 to $15 per child for food and goodie bags, plus another $100 for entertainment, only for a basic birthday party. Scary, isn't it?

The average parents anticipate their child's birthday party with a mixture of happiness and fear. There is no greater embarrassment for a child than having a "boring" birthday party. Parents wrack their brains trying to find new and exciting ways to entertain their children's friends for at least two hours. By the age of nine, many children have gone to clown or magician parties, skating parties, swimming parties, children's museum parties, video arcade parties, movie or home video parties, or fast food restaurant parties. What else is there left to do?

This "one-upmanship" in the staging of children's parties is not only unnecessary, but also potentially harmful. The message that parents are giving their children when they throw extravagant parties is "your friends are only coming because we are throwing this really great party." The message that the birthday child is sending out to his or her friends is "my parents are spending a lot of money on this party." Pity the unfortunate child who cannot keep up with his or her classmates' parties.

There's good news! You don't have to take out a mortgage on your house to provide your child with a great party. By following the simple experiments in this book, and using the reproducible invitations, YOU can create a theme birthday party that your child will always remember. And you won't have to spend a fortune for the entertainment or run yourself ragged.

Any parent can be a successful party host. After all, you entertain your own children almost every day of their lives. Why should a party be any different? The main thing to remember is this: **Read all the experiments that you are going to perform, at least the day before, and collect the few extra items you will need ahead of time.** That way you will feel comfortable with the show.

Now, relax and enjoy yourself. You are about to enter the world of party entertainers.

THIS ISN'T JUST A BIRTHDAY BOOK: PARTIES FOR ALL

These parties are not reserved just for parents planning birthdays. Teachers, youth group leaders, child care workers, and even children's entertainers can use this book to create exciting hands-on activities for any occasion.

Teachers who want to create a special treat for their students can use any of these parties as the basis for a fun and educational day in the classroom. Workstations can be set up on tables where small groups of children can perform separate experiments. The teacher can act as a facilitator in directing the children and answering questions. The children's observations can form the basis of further research projects, reports, and even science fair presentations. Children should be encouraged to record their observations and discuss what happened. Teachers are not limited to one specific party, but can pick and choose from several of the parties.

Teachers and others can involve the children's parents in a special day of party experiments. They can have the child give the parent or caregiver an invitation to a day of fun in the classroom. Each child can lead his or her parent through the experiments and explain to the parent what happened.

WHAT YOU NEED TO KNOW BEFORE THE PARTY

Which Party Is Which?

Take a quiet time, several weeks before your child's birthday, and discuss the type of birthday your child is most interested in. Allow the child to look through the invitations and choose a party that excites him or her the most. Review the activities that you will be doing, and even try a dry run with your child. If your children are older, you might want to get them involved in gathering the materials and testing the experiments.

Picking the Day
(or, Why does my birthday always fall on a Saturday?)

Choose a day and a time to throw the party that is near your child's birthday yet convenient for your household and guests. Throw a small family party on the actual birthday, so that your child doesn't feel that you have forgotten his or her actual birthday.

Christmas Babies, Summer Babies, Holiday Babies. If your child's birthday falls at an inopportune time of the year, like when their friends are away in the summer or during a holiday season, how about throwing a half birthday or unbirthday party instead? This way your child will not feel that he or she has been "cheated" of a great time.

Planning the Party

Invitations. One of the best features of this book is the invitations provided. This saves you the time and expense of looking for an invitation that suits each party's theme. After you have chosen the party, photocopy the appropriate invitation from the book. Fill in the party information, then photocopy the completed invitation. Fold the invitation in half twice, first lengthwise, then across (see diagram to left) and distribute. Invitations are best sent out at least two weeks before the party.

Number of Guests. Every child wants to have a huge birthday party for primarily one reason: By inviting everyone they know, they are guaranteed to receive the greatest number of gifts! From an organizational standpoint, this is a parent's nightmare. Unless you have a huge house, large yard, and a number of helpers, consider having a smaller, more manageable party, with ten or fewer children. If you are determined to have a larger party, definitely get a helper.

Length of the Party. We recommend that parties run for two hours or less. Plan on starting the activities about 15 minutes after the designated starting time. If all the guests arrive on time, you should begin right away.

Materials. You should know how many children will be attending from the invitation's RSVP. This will tell you how many materials you need. We recommend that you carefully read the experiments for the chosen party and have a dry run sometime beforehand so you feel completely comfortable with them. Use the checklist on page *xii* to ensure you have all materials and equipment.

The Day of the Party

When Guests Arrive. While you are waiting for all the children to straggle in, it is a good idea to keep the guests clear of the experiments that you have laid out. If it is a nice day, the children could go outdoors. If it isn't a nice day, or there isn't a suitable place for the children outdoors, then place them in a different room from the one the experiments are in.

A Helper. We recommend that you have an extra pair of hands around for the party to keep you from going crazy. A fellow parent, older sibling, kind neighbor, family friend, or even the baby-sitter can help you keep things firmly in hand. If a child is especially unruly, the helper might assist by controlling the unacceptable behavior or providing an alternative source of entertainment. The helper can also assist in the setup and/or cleanup of experiments.

Photos/Videos. Be sure to have a camera or a video camera and film ready for the party, but face it—you can't do everything! Have your spouse, a close friend, or another parent take the pictures. You'll be too busy!

Food

Most children don't remember the food at parties. They certainly don't appreciate the fact that you spent the better part of yesterday slaving over a hot stove to make a three-course meal. If you decide to serve food, keep it simple—pizza, sandwiches, hot dogs, or vegetables with dip. While festive plates, napkins, cups, and tablecloths are nice, the kids won't enjoy the party any less without them. Save yourself a lot of money and do something nice for the environment—serve on nondisposables. Tell the children you don't think that throwaway dishes are a good idea because of the extra garbage they create. Most children will think this is a wonderful idea.

IMPORTANT: Make sure the kids wash their hands after the experiments, especially if they are going to be eating anything.

To Serve or Not to Serve. An easy solution is to not serve a meal at all. If you decide to do this, then simply call the party for a time that falls between meals, such as 2:00 to 4:00 P.M. This way you can reduce the cost of the party and make life simpler for yourself. You should still have snack foods, such as cake and cookies and drinks.

When to Serve Food. Do not under any circumstances serve food before you do the experiments. Kids tend to get rowdy if you feed them before you begin the experiments. Have healthy snacks (such as vegetables, fruit, and crackers) close by if the crowd gets too jumpy. You can avoid this by having the party begin about one hour after or a few hours before mealtime.

Gifts

Have a laundry hamper, shopping bag, table, or someplace to put the gifts. This keeps them from getting lost, trampled, or damaged.

Opening the Gifts. Some parents make a big production out of opening the gifts. This part of the party is better known as a time filler. It usually takes the birthday child the better part of half an hour to rip through the presents and begin to lose the various pieces.

Something you might want to consider is allowing your child to open the gifts after all the guests have gone home. In this way, your child can appreciate each gift without having it grabbed out of his or her hand by a friend. Some children who go to parties are terrified that the other children will laugh at the gift they have brought. Other children, who cannot afford expensive or showy gifts, feel intimidated and left out during a public open- ing. The best way to save possible hurt feelings and to help your child respect the gifts would be to open all presents in private. If you are looking for things to fill time, check out the "Just in Case" activities in the back of the book, or have the kids play a game until it is time to go. If you have planned the party right, this should only be about ten minutes.

Goodie Bags

It is customary at most birthdays to give out goodie bags. This is what the guests look forward to. It is not necessary to provide expensive and showy giveaways. Goodie bags *need not* be expen- sive to be memorable. One of the neatest things we have seen given out were tiny fir trees wrapped in damp paper towels to take home and plant. Another great idea is to give the children passes to movie theaters or museums. Some of the parties in this book include suggestions for items that can be taken home by the guests.

The contents of the bags should be nearly identical for all guests, so that no one feels that his or her gift is better or worse than someone else's. You may wish to make the girls' and boys' bags different, but the cost should remain the same. THE THING TO REMEMBER IS YOU DO *NOT* HAVE TO SPEND A LOT OF MONEY TO HAVE WONDERFUL GOODIE BAGS.

Other Things You Should Know

The first thing to remember is: *This is fun!* Everyone is here to have a good time. Keep cool. If things go wrong with an experi- ment, or if the experiment doesn't work the way it should—that's okay. Try it again. Not even professionals get everything right every time. Project an aura of confidence. If you believe you're doing great, the kids will believe it, too! You cannot imagine some of the things that have happened to us while we have been doing birthday parties. When something didn't work as expected, we laughed. The kids then laughed. Then we did the experiment once more, and this time—perfection.

The second thing to remember is: *You're the boss!* Kids tend to get excited and lose some of their social graces during parties. Some children may find it hard to listen or may distract others. It is necessary to establish the rules at the beginning of the party. Once all the children are present, you may wish to say something like this:

You probably know me as _____'s mom/dad. But what you don't know about me is that I am also a science performer. We're going to experiment with some really neat things today, but before we do, it's important that you know the ground rules for the party. You must listen very carefully when I'm explaining how to do something. You all can't speak at once. If you wish to ask me a question, you must raise your hand. You might have to take turns asking me questions. If you need help with an experiment, my helper or I will be happy to assist you. And don't taste anything you are experimenting with unless I tell you it's okay. Now we're ready to get started.

Your Reward

No, you won't get nominated for a special award for throwing a great party. What you will get is a special memory and your child's respect for the time and effort you have made to make his or her birthday the best birthday ever!

I'm Still Scared! What Do I Do?

Being an entertainer for children isn't that hard. It's like being with a strange dog: don't show fear! The experiments are easy and you don't have to study for them. It is not necessary to be a comedian. Few of us do this for a living.

If for some reason you feel that you just can't do this—no problem. There are eager science and education students in your area who would love the chance to perform these experiments. Contact the local college, university, or other schools in your area

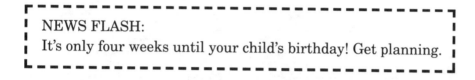

and ask student placement or science or education professors if they can recommend someone. Interview the students and tell them which party or experiments you are interested in. Choose the person you feel would relate best to the kids. Relax. You will be present during the party to supervise the activities. The going rate for students for one of these parties is about $20 to $30. The rates are negotiable depending on the area and the student. And please don't ask the student to get dressed up like a "scientist" unless he or she really wants to.

NEWS FLASH:
It's only four weeks until your child's birthday! Get planning.

PARTY CHECKLIST

The trick behind a successful party is to be organized! One way to do this is to keep a detailed list of things to do. Photocopy this page, fill it in, and check off each item as it is completed.

INVITATIONS: Sent _____ RSVP's _____ Number of Guests Coming _____

SPECIAL INSTRUCTIONS (allergies, dietary restrictions, dislikes, etc.):
_____
_____
_____
_____
_____

Have	Item		Have	Item
__	_____		__	_____
__	_____		__	_____
__	_____		__	_____
__	_____		__	_____
__	_____		__	_____
__	_____		__	_____
__	_____		__	_____
__	_____		__	_____
__	_____		__	_____

LIST OF MATERIALS NEEDED FOR PARTY:

EXPERIMENTS: Read _____ Tried _____

BACKUP EXPERIMENTS:
1. _____ Page _____
2. _____ Page _____
3. _____ Page _____

MATERIALS NEEDED FOR BACKUP:
_____
_____
_____

SUPPLIERS FOR SPECIAL MATERIALS: Name _____ Phone _____
_____ _____

GOODIE BAGS: _____

FOOD LIST:
_____
_____
_____

❐ Plates ❐ Napkins ❐ Cups ❐ Cutlery ❐ Cake ❐ Candles

HELPER: Name _____ Phone _____

xii

❐ Camera ❐ Film ❐ Photographer

Fossils and Dinos

Most children are fascinated by dinosaurs and fossils. While it may not be possible for your party guests to visit a museum with real dino bones, here's an easy way to create your own fossil party. This party allows children to fulfill one of their greatest fantasies by becoming junior archaeologists, while learning how fossils were created.

Ages: 5 to 10
Time: 1 to 1½ hours

MATERIALS

▲ about eight different pictures of dinosaurs

▲ containers (such as yogurt containers or disposable plastic cups), one per child

▲ sand

▲ small rocks, shells, leaves, bones

▲ petroleum jelly

▲ paper towels or rags

▲ plaster of paris (*NOTE:* Do not make ahead of time because it will harden. Do not put down the sink or toilet because it may clog the drain. Throw out in the garbage.)

▲ tempera paints (or food coloring)

▲ pail

▲ small plastic insects or flowers

▲ wax paper or aluminum foil

▲ colorless or amber-colored nail polish (*WARNING:* Nail polish is flammable. Be sure to keep any birthday candles or other flames away from it.)

▲ thick, veiny leaves or fish bones

▲ homemade clay (see page 62) or modeling clay

▲ glass or nonporous rolling pin

▲ Popsicle® sticks

▲ string

▲ spoons

▲ toothbrush

▲ empty plastic mustard bottle

▲ cake mix or homemade cake batter

▲ *optional:* "gummy"-type dinosaur candies

▲ large shells (such as scallops, clams, or oysters)

▲ chocolate chips

▲ *optional:* charcoal briquette powder, olive or vegetable oil, flat rocks, and leaves and/or twigs for paintbrushes

▲ cookie sheet and other cooking utensils

▲ *optional:* a real fossil specimen for goodie bags (These can be purchased in specialty toy shops, museum shops, or through catalogs. The prices range from 50 cents up.)

THINGS TO DO BEFORE THE PARTY

▲ Two weeks before the party, send out the invitations and begin to gather the materials. If your child is a real dinosaur lover, you may wish to gather some of his or her favorite plastic dinos, books, posters, or related items to be used as props for the party. You many want to ask on the invitations that the children come dressed as archaeologists (with khaki shorts, hats, etc.). Let parents know that the kids could get messy.

▲ The day before the party, read the instructions and make certain that you understand the experiments. Review the materials and make sure you have everything. Prepare the clays and containers.

▲ If you are making the fossil cake, you might wish to do this the night before.

▲ The day of the party, set out materials and supplies.

PARTY TIME

In experiments 1, 2, and 3 the children learn about the three types of fossils: fossil casts, amber, and fossil impressions. Experiments 1 and 2 require drying time, and the Chocolate Shells need time to chill in the fridge. A good way to save time is to have the kids make the Chocolate Shells while the plaster is setting (experiment 1), and roll out the clay (experiment 3) while the nail polish is drying (experiment 2). The fruits of experiments 1, 2, and 3 will then be ready at about the same time.

How many of you like dinosaurs? Who can tell me which dinosaur this is? [Hold up a picture of a dino—be sure *you* know which one it is!] *How about this one?* [Try about eight different dinos.] *How do we know if the dino was a meat eater or a plant eater? How do we know so much about dinosaurs and other creatures that lived long ago? We know about these creatures by studying fossils. We're going to be archaeologists and make our own fake fossils.*

1. A Dino in Paris

We can't make a real fossil, because that would take millions of years and special conditions. We can make our own fake fossil casts in a lot less time. What kind of fossil cast would you like to make?

Give each child a small disposable cup with his or her name on it that is ¼ full of sand. Have each child choose an item to "fossilize"—a veiny leaf; a small, bumpy shell; or a chicken bone—and generously coat the item with petroleum jelly. Have the children place their items, bumpy side up, on the sand. Have paper towels or rags handy for messy hands or surfaces.

While the children are doing the above, prepare the plaster of paris or have a helper prepare it. (You may color the plaster of paris with food coloring or tempera paints to produce a colored cast.) When the children are ready, let each child pour or spoon some of the plaster of paris into his or her cup. Set the cups aside until the plaster has hardened (about a half hour). When hard, invert the cup over a pail to catch the sand, and remove the item from the plaster. The result: a plaster cast of the item.

> What, you may ask, is the difference between a *cast* and a *mold*? A mold is made when liquid is poured into a hollow container and allowed to harden into the shape of the container's interior. A cast is made by pouring plaster around the outside of an object and letting the plaster harden.

2. An Experiment That Resinates

How many of you have ever looked closely at a fir or pine tree? [Option: If you happen to have a pine tree nearby, you may wish to gather some resin by either making a small cut in the side of the tree or scraping some of the existing resin off the tree to show the children.] *Have you ever seen or felt the gooey, yellow stuff on the side of the tree? This is called "resin." What do you think would happen if an insect landed on this stuff? Many prehistoric insects and other very small creatures have been found enclosed in resin, or "amber" as it is called. After many years the resin hardens around these creatures and perfectly saves or preserves them. Some people wear*

Let each child choose a small, plastic insect or a flower petal. Place the object on wax paper or aluminum foil and slowly drip nail polish over the object, one drop at a time. Do not apply too much at a time, as it will take longer to dry. To save time and the children's patience, let each child apply one or two drops, then pass the bottle to the next person. When each object is completely covered with polish, label it with the child's name and set it aside to dry. This may take about 15 minutes or more, depending on how much polish was used. These "amber" fossils can be glued onto an inexpensive pendant and worn as a necklace.

3. An Impressive Experiment

Now that we have created a fossil cast and an amber fossil, let's create an impression of an item. This is the form of an object as it appears when it is pressed into a soft substance. Dinosaur tracks are preserved in a similar way.

Have each child gather or select a thick, veiny leaf or, if possible, the cleaned bones of a small fish (such as a trout or salmon). Give each child enough modeling clay so that it can be rolled out wider than the object. Place the object, bumpy side down, on the clay and cover with wax paper. Let the children press the item with their fingers into the clay to create an impression. Remove the wax paper, gently peel off the item, and let the clay harden.

4. Dig This

Let's go outside and see if we can find fossils like archaeologists do. Archaeologists find fossils in many places around the world by digging in hardened earth. Most fossils are found under deep layers of soil that have piled on top of them, protecting the fossils for centuries.

If you have a garden, sandbox, or a suitable outdoor space where children can dig, you might try an outdoor hunt. Before the children arrive, create an area for each child to dig. Do this by placing Popsicle sticks in the ground to mark off an area about 18×18 inches $(45 \times 45$ cm$)$ and tying string around the sticks to enclose each square. Allow one square for each child. Bury objects such as bones, fake fossils, and so on in the loose soil or sand.

When you are ready to take the children outside for this game, give each one a spoon and tell him or her to choose one of the marked-off squares. Then have the children start digging carefully. When a fossil is found, you can show the child how to remove the dirt surrounding the fossil using a small toothbrush and/or squeezing the air through the spout of an empty plastic mustard bottle. Tell them that real archaeologists must be very gentle when removing soil from fossils so that the fossils don't break. The fossil can then be labeled with the area in which it was found and the name of the child who found it and placed in a box.

5. Optional Recipes

Here are some recipes to add fun to your dino party. For children age nine and over, you could let them make Chocolate Shells to garnish the cake (or just to eat on their own) following the recipe below. Provide younger children with icing and ice cream to decorate the cake.

Fossil Cake

If you're really ambitious, you might want to try to bake a Fossil Cake the night before the party. Prepare your favorite cake recipe, or follow the instructions on a store-bought cake mix. You might need a double recipe depending on the number of guests. Add some "gummy"-type candies shaped like dinosaurs to the batter. Generously grease and flour the bottom and sides of a large glass baking dish or a roasting pan. Grease the bumpy sides of the large, clean shells (scallops), and place them, bumpy sides up, in the pan. Gently pour the batter over the shells and bake according to the instructions in your recipe or on the cake mix package. After removing the cake from the oven, gently invert it on a cake rack to cool. Carefully peel away the shells. At the party, let the children fill the "casts" of the shells with icing and garnish with Chocolate Shells (recipe below).

Chocolate Shells

Melt chocolate chips in a bowl over hot water, adding 1 table-spoon (15 ml) of butter or whipping cream to the mixture. When the mixture is cool but not hard, paint the bumpy side of clean shells with the chocolate mixture, and place the shells, chocolate side up, on a cookie sheet. Put the cookie sheet in the fridge. When the chocolate has hardened, it should fall away from the shell, leaving a chocolate fossil cast that the children can decorate the cake with or take home in goodie bags.

When you serve the cake (after the experiments!), tell the children to imagine they are archaeologists hunting fossils, then watch the surprised looks on their faces when they find a "gummy" dinosaur on their forks.

If the children are young, or if you don't want to use chocolate, let the children make rock paintings instead. (See the "Barbeque Paint" experiment on page 21 of the "Color Your World" party.)

It's a
_____
party!

for:_____
date:_____
time:_____
place:_____
please bring:_____

R.S.V.P.

_____

Mad Scientists

Every child associates science with mixing liquids to cause a reaction, preferably an explosive one! Here's a fun party that will allow them to do just that!

Ages: 7 to 12

Time: approximately 1 hour

MATERIALS

▲ plastic cups (two per child)
▲ plastic spoons (two per child)
▲ food coloring
▲ white vinegar
▲ baking soda
▲ dishwashing liquid
▲ *optional:* empty wine bottle with cork
▲ scissors
▲ aluminum foil
▲ tall glass jar
▲ washing soda (available at grocery stores)
▲ pencil
▲ candle
▲ any laxative containing phenolphthalein (Ex-Lax®, Feen-a-mint®)
▲ rubbing alcohol
▲ bar of white soap
▲ three water glasses
▲ bleach
▲ sugar
▲ string
▲ plastic paper clips
▲ straws
▲ flavorings (such as almond or vanilla extract)
▲ plastic wrap
▲ cardboard or postcard

THINGS TO DO BEFORE THE PARTY

▲ Two weeks before the party, send out the invitations and begin to gather the materials.
▲ The day before the party, try out the experiments, making sure that you have all the materials.
▲ The day of the party, set out the materials. An hour or two before the party, make the Supersaturated Sugar Solution for experiment 5.

Always have a damp cloth handy and some paper towels in case of spills. It's a good idea to protect the table and floor by covering them with a canvas or plastic drop cloth. If it is a nice day, you can do the experiments outdoors in a shady area.

PARTY TIME

Who knows what scientists do? There are many different types of scientists. Biologists study living things. Physicists study how things move. Botanists study plants. Today we're going to be chemists. Chemists study substances and what happens when substances are mixed or changed. These are called "chemical reactions."

Today we are going to be mad scientists and experiment with different chemicals. The important thing to remember is: Don't taste any of the mixtures that we concoct during our party! Now, get ready to have fun.

1. Volcanoes

We can't go to Hawaii to watch a volcano erupt, but we can create our own volcano blast right here.

The children should stand, rather than sit, around the table for this experiment. Give each child a plastic cup and spoon. Pass red food coloring around the table, and have each child add several drops of coloring to the cup. Fill each child's cup about ⅓ full with white vinegar. Let the birthday child go first and then each child around the table take a turn. Have each child add one heaping spoonful (15 ml) of baking soda to the cup, then stand back and watch the chemical reaction.

Have a big bowl in the middle of the table to dump the volcanoes into. Have the kids try the experiment again (with the same cups and spoons), this time adding a drop of dishwashing liquid before the children add the baking soda. Kids love watching their friends' volcanoes erupt.

This experiment can also be done with a loosely

corked bottle. Pour the vinegar into an old wine bottle and then add the baking soda to it. Quickly push a cork loosely into the mouth of the bottle and watch as the cork pops off. You have to be very fast to do this right, and make sure the cork is not pointed at anyone's face.

2. Get a Bang out of This

How can we get a jar of water to make noise? Let's see if we can make this jar of water go bang!

A. Have the children cut aluminum foil into small squares about the size of a quarter (approximately 15 pieces altogether). Let them drop these pieces into a tall glass jar. Have an adult fill the jar with boiled water. Add 3 tablespoons (45 ml) of washing soda to the water. With an adult's assistance, let the children cover the top of the jar with aluminum foil and fold the foil around the rim to make a tight-fitting cover.

Using a sharpened pencil, poke a small hole in the center of the foil. Watch closely as the foil pieces magically rise to the surface and bubbles form. After two minutes, hold the end of a lit candle directly over the hole in the foil and wait for the noise. After each "explosion," readjust the foil for a snug fit. Don't be alarmed if a flame appears over the hole. The flame and the pop are caused by the combustion of hydrogen gas. The hydrogen gas was created by the reaction between the aluminum foil, the washing soda, and the hot water.

B. Have the children remove the aluminum foil lid and pour some dishwashing liquid into the water. Stir the detergent into the water and place a lit candle over the bubbles. Watch the amazement of the children as the bubbles go bang, bang, bang!

3. Vampire Blood

This experiment is just like magic! Have you ever wondered how a magician changes the color of liquids? Here's one way how. But, remember, we can't drink any of these mixtures!

Crush two tablets of any laxative containing phenolphthalein (but not chocolate flavored) and add a tablespoon (15 ml) of rubbing alcohol to the powder. Rub this paste on the children's hands and blow them until they are dry. Hand the children a wet bar of white soap. (NOTE: The soap must be white or the trick won't work.) You may want to have a camera handy to capture the expression on the children's faces when they see fuchsia soap flowing from their hands. The chemical in the laxative reacted with the soap to create this colorful effect.

4. Color Change

Here's another way a magician changes the color of liquids.

Have two glasses ½ full of water. When the children are not looking, add 3 tablespoons (45 ml) of bleach to one of the glasses. To the other glass add 3 to 4 drops of red food coloring. Slowly begin pouring the bleach water into the red water. The red water will turn clear right before your eyes. The bleach dissolves the red color, causing the red water to become clear. Add some more red food coloring to the bleach water and watch as the color dissolves into nothing and the water remains clear.

The glass of clear water contains bleach which reacted with the red coloring. This is why bleach is used to get stains out of laundry.

Be sure to keep the bleach and bleach water out of the children's reach and dispose of the bleach water as soon as this experiment is over.

5. Amazing Sugar Crystals

This is a take-home experiment because it takes a few days for the sugar crystals to harden into rock candy.

An hour or two before the party, make the Supersaturated Sugar Solution. Boil 16 cups (4 liters) of water in a large stockpot. While stirring, slowly add sugar until no more sugar will dissolve. Put this solution aside until party time.

At the party, give each child a plastic cup and spoon, a piece of string, a straw, and a plastic paper clip. Pour each child's cup ¾ full with the sugar solution. Have on the table a selection of flavorings, such as almond or vanilla extract, and food colorings so that the children can color and flavor their sugar crystals. Let each child tie the paper clip to one end of the string. Lay the straw across the mouth of the cup and tie the string to the middle of the straw so that the plastic paper clip is suspended in the solution but does not touch the bottom of the cup. Cover the cup tightly with plastic wrap so the children can take this treat home without spilling it.

Tell them to put the cup in an out-of-the-way spot at home, remove the plastic wrap, and keep checking the cup until the sugar crystals have hardened around the string. They will have made their own rock candy.

> FOOD IDEA: The morning of the party, place stalks of celery in water colored with food coloring. Just before the party, slice the celery diagonally and serve colored celery.

6. Not a Drop of Water

Make sure that this experiment is done over the sink or a bowl because there may be some spills.

What do you think would happen if I turned this glass of water upside down? Do you think that it would make a difference if I put this piece of paper on top? I need a volunteer to help me.

Fill a glass of water to the rim and add food coloring. Have a child place a square piece of thick paper, such as a postcard or cardboard, over the top of the glass. While holding the cardboard in place, quickly turn the glass upside down. The air pressure will keep the water inside the glass, making it look like the paper is holding the water in the glass.

It's a

_____

party!

for:_____
date:_____
time:_____
place:_____
please bring:_____

R.S.V.P.

_____

Color Your World

Ages: 4 to 8

Time: approximately 1 hour

Creating your own paints, prints, and dyes is loads of fun! Making their very own paints and prints allows children to be very creative in color and design. It is very easy to do and fun for both adults and children. This is a wonderful party to have outdoors on a sunny day, and it is perfect for young children.

MATERIALS

▲ tempera paints (powdered or liquid)

▲ saucepans

▲ cornstarch

▲ heavy paper

▲ several picture books on art (your own or from a library)

▲ liquid starch

▲ *optional:* sand, glitter, salt, talcum powder, and/or coffee grounds; spices (such as cinnamon) or perfume

▲ unsweetened powdered drink mix (such as Kool-Aid®)

▲ cooking pots with lids

▲ white vinegar

▲ lidded bowls or jars

▲ white cotton or cotton/polyester blend T-shirts

▲ string or rubber bands

▲ empty dishwashing liquid bottles

▲ spoons

▲ newspaper

▲ pencil crayons or regular crayons

▲ fresh leaves and/or flowers

▲ white paper

▲ watercolors

▲ charcoal powder (from the bottom of a bag of charcoal briquettes)

▲ olive or vegetable oil

▲ flat rocks

▲ *optional:* scraps of leather or canvas

▲ leaves and/or twigs, or paintbrushes

THINGS TO DO BEFORE THE PARTY

▲ Two weeks before the party, send out invitations. Tell the parents to dress their children in play clothes or things they won't mind getting paint on. Begin to gather the materials.

▲ The day before the party, read the instructions and make sure that you have all the materials. Make the dyes for tie-dyeing.

▲ The day of the party, set out the materials and prepare the paints.

PARTY TIME

Today we are going to be artists and create our own paints and pictures. Did you know that long ago artists would mix special paints? This way they could get just the color and texture of paint they wanted. There is a color called "Titian red," named after an artist who liked a special shade of red. If you were an artist, what color would you like to have named after you? Today you can make that color.

Artists paint pictures in different ways. Some artists paint pictures that look so real it seems that the object is right in front of you, while others paint an interpretation of how they think the object looks. One painter named Jackson Pollock created pictures that looked like drips of color on the paper. Another, named Picasso, made pictures that looked as if the objects were made from geometric shapes. [Show the children a selection of pictures and ask their opinions on which ones they like or dislike.]

Making Paints

1. Quick and Easy Finger Paint

NOTE: Plan to make the paints about ½ hour before the party, or if the children are older, you can involve them in the process.

A. All you need for this activity is water, powdered or liquid tempera paint, saucepans, and cornstarch. For each color, bring 6 cups (1.5 liters) of water to a boil and remove it from the heat. Mix 2 cups (500 ml) of cornstarch into a little cool water and add it to the hot water, stirring all the time. Put the mixture back on the heat and boil it until it is clear and thick (one to two minutes). Add the tempera paint (as much as necessary to achieve the desired color). Let the paint cool, but use it when it is slightly warm. Use the paint on heavy paper. That is all you need to do to make great finger paint!

Ask the children to use the paint to create a picture in the same style as their favorite artist, or have them copy a picture of, say, *Sunflowers* by van Gogh. Place the art somewhere safe, so that it can be taken home at the end of the party.

B. This recipe is even easier than the first one. You will need liquid starch, heavy paper (such as standard-size construction paper), and liquid or powdered tempera paint. First, take a damp cloth and moisten the paper to make a slippery surface. Then, pour a puddle of liquid starch (about 1 tablespoon, 15 ml) on the heavy paper. Add a tablespoon (15 ml) or so of paint to the middle of the starch and mix. Have the children spread the mixture around with their fingers.

To add texture to the paint, add sand, glitter, salt, talcum powder, or coffee grounds. Add scents like cinnamon or other spices, perfume, or even essential oils to create scratch-and-sniff art.

Have the children paint a picture of a flower that really smells like a flower, or a picture of a woman that smells like perfume. You can even have the children do an abstract picture, using scents and texture to suggest the subject matter. Let the other children guess what it is a picture of.

2. Tie-Dyeing

Kids of all ages love to wear tie-dyed T-shirts or other clothing. This experiment is very simple and fun to do at a home party. It also makes a lasting gift the children can take home and wear. Inexpensive white T-shirts are easy to find at any clothing store.

Many years ago—not quite as long ago as when dinosaurs roamed the earth, but close—people who wore tie-dyed clothes were considered "cool." Do you know when tie-dye first became popular? In the 1960s. How many years ago was that? Let's bring back some childhood memories for your parents and make our own tie-dyed shirts. When you get home today, you can say, "Hey, man. Doesn't this look groovy?"

The day before the party, make the dye. The best dye is made from powdered drink mix, such as Kool-Aid® (yes, Kool-Aid®!). You will need several flavors of unsweetened drink mix (the deep colors work the best—purple, blue, green, red, and orange), cooking pots with lids, white vinegar, water, and lidded jars or bowls to store the paints. Pour two packages of drink mix into the cooking pot (use a different color in each pot) and add ½ cup (125 ml) of white vinegar and ½ cup (125 ml) of water to each pot.

Cover the pots and simmer until the liquid is steaming. Continue to simmer for 20 to 30 minutes. Let the liquids cool, then pour them into the storage containers. This dye should keep for several weeks if refrigerated. Make sure to mark it "DYE" so that no one drinks it.

At the party, dye the T-shirts. Put the different colored dyes into bowls or in empty dishwashing liquid bottles. Fold the T-shirts into small squares, triangles, rectangles, or diamonds, or twist them up. Secure them with string or rubber bands. To apply the dye, squeeze it out of the dishwashing liquid bottles, spoon it out of the bowl, or simply dip parts of the shirt into each color of dye. Next, remove the string or the rubber bands, unfold or untwist the T-shirts and lay them flat to dry. Have a helper iron the shirts dry, or if this isn't possible, send the shirts home with instructions to the parents to finish drying the shirts. The T-shirts should be ironed before the first washing and always washed in cold water to retain the color.

3. Nature Rubbings and Prints

In different places in Europe, people visit old churches and make things called "brass rubbings." A large sheet of dark paper is taped over an ancient brass plate that has an engraved image on it, and a gold or silver crayon is rubbed over the paper until the image shows through. These pictures are usually of knights or ladies. Since we can't go to Europe for the afternoon, we're going to create our own rubbings using some common things we can find in the neighborhood.

Nature rubbings and prints are great fun. All the children have to do is go outside into your backyard or nearby park and choose natural objects to use in their artwork. Once they've collected the materials, these activities can be done either indoors or outdoors.

A. Rubbings are very easy to do. All you need is a newspaper, pencil crayons or regular crayons, fresh green leaves or flowers, and white paper. Any leaf will work if its veins are easy to see. First, spread out the newspaper where the children are going to work. Have the children spread the leaves or flowers over the newspaper and cover them with a sheet of white paper. Then tell them to hold the crayon sideways and rub it over the paper until a print of the leaves or flowers appears on the paper. After creating designs on the paper with crayons, the children can paint the rest of the paper with watercolors, which will not color the rubbing because of the wax in the crayon.

B. Nature prints are also a very easy and creative activity. Use fresh green leaves, tempera paints, newspaper, and white or light-colored paper. Spread out the newspaper and have the children arrange the leaves in a design on top. Ask the children to paint the textured side of the leaves with colored paint and then lay the white paper on top of the leaves. Then tell them to slide one hand under the newspaper and, with the other hand, gently press the white paper so that the paint on the leaves goes onto the white paper. Have the children remove the white paper, peel off the leaves, and lay the paper flat to dry. You can also use flowers that have been pressed flat or any flat object.

4. Barbecue Paint

How would you like to create paintings like cave dwellers did? Prehistoric people used to paint on cave walls using some sort of charcoal paint. We are going to make and use a similar kind of paint.

Collect the powder that's left in the bottom of a bag of charcoal briquettes. For every tablespoon (15 ml) of powder, have the children mix in an equal amount of olive or other vegetable oil. Gather some flat rocks (or have the children do this), or use old scraps of leather or canvas. Tell the children to paint them with the barbecue paint using brushes made from leaves or twigs (or actual paintbrushes).

It's a
_____
party!

for:_____
date:_____
time:_____
place:_____
please bring:_____

R.S.V.P.

_____

I Spy

Children love to play spy. The challenge of solving crimes or hunting imaginary criminals is fun for kids of all ages. This party not only allows the guests to become famous detectives, but also gives you the chance to explain the science behind spy gadgets like invisible ink and chromatography.

Ages: 5 and up

Time: approximately 1½ hours

MATERIALS

▲ lemons or lemon juice (juice of ½ lemon per child)

▲ cups

▲ cotton swabs or toothpicks

▲ paper

▲ lamp with 100-watt light bulb

▲ water-soluble dark-colored felt markers (from different manufacturers)

▲ paper coffee filters or paper towels

▲ water glasses

▲ pencils (pairs of different widths)

▲ ink pads

▲ notebook and loose-leaf paper

▲ facial tissues or rags

▲ talcum powder

▲ cocoa powder

▲ plastic bags

▲ inexpensive magnifying glasses (about 25 cents each)

▲ old hardcover books (from used book stores or rummage sales)

▲ scissors

▲ white glue

▲ cardboard

THINGS TO DO BEFORE THE PARTY

▲ Two weeks before the party, send out the invitations and begin to gather the materials. You might suggest to the parents that the kids come dressed as their favorite detective or spy. (How many budding Sherlock Holmeses, James Bonds, or Mata Haris do you think will show up?)

▲ The day before the party, read the instructions and make sure that you have all the materials. Using one of the dark-colored felt markers, prepare the sample rainbow for experiment 2.

▲ The day of the party, set out the materials. Prepare the coffee filter strips for experiment 2 and the books for experiment 5.

PARTY TIME

1. Invisible Ink

Ever wonder how the Invisible Man writes a letter? He uses invisible ink! Here's how you can write your own secret messages.

Slice a lemon in half and squeeze the juice into a cup. You will need the juice of about ½ lemon per child. Have each child dip the end of a toothpick or swab ("pen") into the lemon juice ("ink") and write a secret message on a piece of paper. When the lemon juice dries, it is invisible. To decode the secret message, simply hold the paper close to a lighted bulb. The heat will cause the lemon juice to brown, and the message will appear as if by miracle.

2. Paper Chromatography

Some mysterious person has written me a secret message and I need you to help me discover who did it.

The day before the party, prepare a sample rainbow using one of the dark-colored felt markers. Put the marker back with the other markers. At the party, show the children the sample rainbow and ask them to try to guess which marker made the rainbow. Let each child choose a different dark-colored marker, making sure that one child gets the same marker you used. Give each child one strip of a coffee filter or paper towel that has been cut into strips about ½ inch wide (1.25 cm) and 4 to 5 inches (12 to 13 cm) long. Have each child make a mark on the strip about 2 inches (5 cm) from the end with the marker. Put 1 inch (2.5 cm) of water in a glass. Ask each child to place his or her strip in the glass so that the ink mark is above the water. Wait for the strip to absorb the water. When the water reaches the ink, rainbowlike colors will appear along the strip. Compare rainbows and see whose rainbow comes closest to the sample. Give a prize to the child who had the mystery pen.

Felt markers are made from different color combinations. Each manufacturer uses different amounts of primary colored inks to create its pens. That is why a brown marker from company A is a darker brown than the same color marker from company B. As the colors separate in the water, you can see the colors that were used to make the color. Chromatography is the process of separating the colors.

3. Secret Codes

You are a spy in another country and you want to send a message to your government. Your job is to create a secret code that cannot be read by prying eyes.

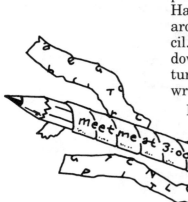

Group the children in pairs so that each pair has two identical pencils whose widths are different from those of the other pairs. Have each child cut a thin piece of paper and wrap it tightly around his or her pencil. Tape the ends of the paper to the pencil. Each child can then write a secret message or code word down the length of the pencil. (The partners will have to take turns using each other's pencils to write messages on their wrapped pencils.)

Have the child fill in the rest of the paper with any other letters. When the paper is unwrapped, it looks like nonsense. Have each partner try to decode the spy friend's message by wrapping it around his or her own pencil. The code can only be broken if the paper is wrapped around a pencil of the same width.

4. Who Stole the Cookie from the Cookie Jar?

Master detectives! We need your help to solve a mystery. As you know, no two people's fingerprints are the same. On the wall you will see a set of fingerprints that were found on the cookie jar. See if you can discover who they belong to and solve the mystery of the missing cookie!

When the guests arrive, fingerprint each child by pressing his or her thumb on an ink pad, then onto the page of a notebook. Wipe each child's thumb clean using a facial tissue or rag.

Randomly choose one print and set it aside. When it is time for this experiment, hang up this fingerprint. Repeat the finger-printing, labeling each print with the child's name. Hang up all the prints. Have the children compare the prints and choose the fingerprint that is the closest to the sample print. All the children, including the owner of the sample fingerprints, should get a prize for solving the mystery—how about some cookies!

5. Take-Home Fingerprint Kit

If the kids liked that last experiment, they'll love this take-home gift.

Place 2 tablespoons (30 ml) of talcum powder in one plastic bag and 2 tablespoons (30 ml) of cocoa powder in another plastic bag. Give each child the bags to take home, along with the following instructions (which you can copy from the book or write out yourself):

> Dip a finger into the powder, then roll the finger over a smooth surface (such as a glass, mirror, or some other shiny object). Take a small piece of transparent tape and carefully lay it over the fingerprint. Quickly peel the tape off and put the tape onto a piece of paper (white paper for a cocoa print, dark paper for a talcum print). If you wish, you can study the print with a magnifying glass.

You could also include an inexpensive magnifying glass for the children to take home. These are available for about 25 cents in most toy or novelty shops.

6. Secret Book

NOTE: This activity is for children who can safely handle scissors and competently glue paper. If the guests are younger children, you can make these books ahead of time and give them out as take-home gifts, or you can precut the books using an X-acto knife and have the children glue the books at the party.

We all know that books can contain many secrets. How about a book that holds your own secret letters and messages? What do you think this would look like? Have you ever seen a movie about spies? Did they have a special place for hiding things? Where was it?

Have each child select one of the old books you have collected for this activity. Have the child open the book about halfway and draw an outline about 1 inch (2.5 cm) to 2 inches (5 cm) away from the edge of each page (see diagram). Have each child use scissors and a ruler to cut the page along the outline. Several pages at a time can be cut. Cut or fold cardboard to line the hole, and glue it to the pages to keep them from flipping, Remember also to glue the back cover to the last page so that nothing will fall out. Use a type of glue that dries clear. Set books aside until the end of the party.

It's a

_____

party!

for:_____
date:_____
time:_____
place:_____
please bring: _____

R.S.V.P.

_____

Paper and Sculpting

Ages: 6 to 9

Time: approximately 1½ hours

If you have a rec room (or maybe a wreck room), or a nice place to hold this party outdoors, try the following entertainment. It's messy and it will take some patience, but it's great fun and the kids will never forget it. Remember to cover the floors and tables with newspapers or drop cloths.

MATERIALS

▲ colored tissue paper, facial tissues, or crepe paper
▲ old bowl or plastic container
▲ liquid starch
▲ white glue
▲ small boxes, empty clean milk cartons, or bottles
▲ glitter, sand, or confetti
▲ *optional:* picture book of the solar system and nylon fishing line or string
▲ plaster of paris
▲ food coloring, tempera paints, or glow-in-the-dark paints
▲ balloons (one per child)
▲ funnel or the top half of a plastic soda bottle
▲ plastic bucket
▲ alum (available at most drug stores or grocery stores)
▲ coat hangers
▲ old sheets, pillowcases, or towels
▲ latex gloves (one pair per child)
▲ flour or wallpaper paste
▲ salt
▲ small flat rocks
▲ blow-dryer
▲ paint sets (one per child)

THINGS TO DO BEFORE THE PARTY

▲ Two weeks before the party, send out the invitations. Ask the children to wear old clothes, not good party clothes, as the experiments are messy! Start gathering the glues, paints, varnishes, paper, balloons, stones, and other items for the party.
▲ The day before the party, make sure you have all the materials. Prepare the glues and paints.
▲ The day of the party, set out the materials.

PARTY TIME

Papier-mâché objects are great fun to make, but the traditional method of sculpting with this material is time consuming, labor intensive, and generally requires several days or even weeks to finish the drying, painting, and clear coating! Have no fear! You don't have to keep guests at your house for the better part of a week.

Set up workstations so that children can choose the types of sculpting they wish to try.

1. Tissue Sculpture

Today we are going to create sculptures using tissue paper. Who has always wanted their own star or planet? Well, you can make one of your very own to hang in your room.

Before the party, collect colored tissue paper. You can either save the wrappings from clothes or breakables, or ask for some in a department store or boutique. You could also use colored facial tissues or even crepe paper.

Let the children rip the paper into bits or strips and place them in an old bowl or plastic container. Cover the strips with liquid starch (available at most grocery stores), and let sit for about five minutes. Add enough white glue (the type kids use in school) to make a gooey mixture. Have the children pull the strips of paper through their fingers to remove some of the liquid and then apply the strips to objects such as small boxes, empty milk cartons, or even bottles. If you used colored paper, painting will not be necessary. Let the children sprinkle glitter, sand, confetti, or other textured items on their creations to give them that something special.

To make this a science activity, you can have the children create their own solar system mobiles. Have the children make planet-shaped spheres, using pictures of the planets from a book or poster as models. When dry, "planets" can be painted, then attached to coat hangers using nylon fishing line or string. Create moons or even meteors and paint them with glow-in-the-dark paints (available at most toy or hobby shops).

2. Paris Weights

Let's make something that will keep our papers from flying away in the wind. We will be using something called "plaster of paris." Does anyone know what that is? Plaster of paris does not come only from Paris, France. It now comes from the hardware store down the street. It's a special material that doctors once used to make casts when people broke their arms or legs. Plaster of paris is made from something called "gypsum." The strangest thing happens to plaster of paris when it is drying. Do you know what that is? It gets hotter when it begins to dry. This is called an "exothermic" reaction. You'll be able to feel the heat yourself by holding the balloon as the plaster dries.

> *NOTE:* Do not put leftover plaster of paris down the sink or toilet, because it may clog the drain. Throw any extra in the garbage.

Make a drippy batch of plaster of paris according to the instructions on the package. Add food coloring or tempera paints to the plaster while it is wet. Give each child a balloon, and let the child or a helper hold the balloon while you pour the runny plaster through a funnel into the balloon. (If you don't want to ruin a funnel, you can cut a plastic soda bottle in half and put the balloon over the spout.) Tie the balloon tightly. The children can create weird shapes by holding or squeezing the balloon until the plaster begins to harden. When the balloon is firm, let it dry. To paint their creations, the children can leave the plaster in the balloon or peel off the balloon.

3. Halloween Ghosts

Who would like their own pet ghost or other creature? Let's make one.

If you're having an October party, you might want to get kids into a spooky mood with this experiment. If you don't want to make ghost shapes, you could make animals or dinos, or just let the kids decide for themselves.

In an old plastic bucket or container, mix 5 cups (1.25 liters) of plaster of paris, 5 tablespoons (75 ml) of alum, and 5 cups (1.25 liters) of water. Add more water if necessary to make the mixture runny. Have the children bend a wire coat hanger into a strange or scary shape. Cut circles or squares out of old sheets, pillowcases, or towels and soak them in plaster of paris. Place the dripping material over the hangers and leave it to dry. This won't take long, so the children will have to work quickly. As the "ghosts" harden, the children can continue to shape or mold them.

Make sure that the children wash their hands immediately after using the plaster. It is a good idea to have them wear cheap latex gloves, such as those found in paint stores. After the shape has dried, the kids can paint on faces or other details using glow-in-the-dark paints or any water-soluble paints.

4. Paper Rocks

Do you think a piece of paper can keep a door open? Let's make a paper doorstop.

Have each child select or find a small flat rock (about the size of a hamburger). Let the children rip up used white or colored paper or newsprint. Prepare a paste using wallpaper paste or by mixing 1 cup (250 ml) of water, 1 cup (250 ml) of flour, several tablespoons (about 75 ml) of salt, and a squeeze of white glue. (This is where it gets really messy.) Have the children dip their hands into the paste and smother their rocks in paste, then wrap the paper around the rocks and add more paste to smooth out the surface. Have the children shape their rocks by adding layers of paper in different ways (crumpled, rolled, etc.). They could also add another rock to these layers to create a multilevel doorstop. When the children are finished, blow-dry the rocks.

> If you have extra time, have the children paint their rocks as whatever animal they think it resembles. If you are running out of time, send the kids home with their rocks and an inexpensive paint set (available at most toy stores for under a dollar).

PAPER AND SCULPTING PARTY

It's a
_____
party!

for:_____
date:_____
time:_____
place:_____
please bring:_____

R.S.V.P.

_____

6

Bubble Blast

Ages: 6 and up

Time: approximately 1 hour

What child of any age can resist making bubbles? Here's a perfect way to throw a hands-on party at very little cost. Bubble parties are also wonderful for adult gatherings. One of the silliest parties we've thrown was for a group of teachers who wanted to learn to play with bubbles! If you've ever gone to a science show at a hands-on museum, the "bubblology" display was probably the most popular. Here's a foolproof way to have your own show, right in your own backyard.

MATERIALS

- ▲ dishwashing liquid (several different types)
- ▲ glycerin
- ▲ corn syrup
- ▲ bowls (one per three children)
- ▲ plastic tablecloth or plastic table
- ▲ plastic drinking straws
- ▲ cone-shaped paper cups
- ▲ toilet paper or paper towel rolls
- ▲ wire coat hangers
- ▲ piece of garden hose or screen
- ▲ masking tape
- ▲ felt pen
- ▲ string
- ▲ several rulers
- ▲ store-bought bubble wands
- ▲ plastic cups
- ▲ tempera paints (three different colors)
- ▲ paper
- ▲ paper clips
- ▲ watch with a second hand
- ▲ *optional:* lidded glass jars
- ▲ protractor
- ▲ water glasses
- ▲ *optional:* toddler pool, four plastic ties, and a hula hoop or a piece of PVA tubing and joiners cut to make a hoop
- ▲ *optional:* balloon

NOTE: "Bubble Blast" can be a messy party so be prepared! Have several washcloths and buckets of water on hand.

THINGS TO DO BEFORE THE PARTY

- ▲ Two weeks before the party, send out the invitations and begin to gather the materials.
- ▲ The day before the party, review the experiments and make sure you have all the materials.
- ▲ The day of the party, set out all the materials.

PARTY TIME

Most of you probably think of bubbles as fun, but bubble making is also a science. We're going to make some radical bubbles and learn something about the reasons they hold together. Something that you have to know: If you need to rub your eyes, make sure that your hands are clean and dry. If you have bubble solution on your hands, don't put your fingers in your mouth, and don't rub your eyes. Most important: Don't blow bubbles at other children.

Bubble Brew recipe

Make a bowl of Bubble Brew for every three children to share.

½ cup (125 ml) dishwashing liquid (Joy works best)

1 cup (250 ml) water

¼ cup (60 ml) glycerin

¼ cup (60 ml) corn syrup

1. Handmade Bubbles!

Did you know that each of you was born with a bubble blower? Where do you think it is hidden? Is it your mouth? Not really, although your mouth is part of it. Give up? It's your hands!

Get each child to dip his or her hand in the Bubble Brew. Tell the child to make a fist and slowly open it to make a circle with their index finger and thumb. There should be a film of bubble solution inside the circle. Have the child slowly and gently blow into the circle to make bubbles. Ask the children to keep blowing bubbles this way without dipping into the bubble solution again until they can't make any more bubbles.

2. Half a Bubble

You just made a bubble shaped like a circle. How do you think you could make just half a bubble?

Pour a thin layer of Bubble Brew onto the center of the table and smear it around for a moment. Give each child a straw. Have each child dip the end of the straw into the brew and hold it just above the tabletop and blow gently. A bubble will begin to form. Tell the children to keep blowing and see how big a half bubble they can make. What happens if the children touch the bubble with a dry straw? A wet straw? Make a large bubble on the table and have all the children put their wet straws into the bubble and gently blow. See how large a bubble they can make.

> TRICK: You can blow a bubble the size of the table. Wet the table and your hands with Bubble Brew. With the thumb and index finger of both hands, make a circle, stretching a film of bubble solution inside the circle. Starting with your hands near the tabletop, gently blow through the circle to make a bubble on the table. Slowly raise your hands to create a giant bubble. Close the bubble by squeezing your fingers shut.

3. Bubble Inside a Bubble

Has anyone seen a balloon inside a balloon? How do you think you could get a bubble inside a bubble?

Using the same technique as experiment 2, blow a bubble on the table. Take a straw and dip it into the Bubble Brew, making sure that some of the brew stays inside the straw. Gently put the wet end of the straw through the bubble and slowly blow. Another bubble should form inside the first. Have each child try to make his or her own bubble inside a bubble.

4. Making Bubble Makers

What kinds of bubble makers can you create? What materials and shapes do you think will work best?

Have the children make other bubble blowing tools out of materials you supply. You can use almost anything that has a hole through it. Try having them make a bubble trumpet by cutting the bottom off a cone-shaped paper cup. Have the children dip the large end of the cone into the brew, take it out, and blow slowly. A cardboard roll from toilet paper or paper towels also works well. Another excellent tool is a wire coat hanger bent into the shape of a loop with a handle. The coat hanger wand makes large, strong bubbles. You can also use pieces of garden hose or anything else that has holes in it, such as a piece of screen. Using masking tape and a felt pen, label the blowers with the child's name.

5. Big Bubbles!

Who can blow the biggest bubble? How about the smallest? How about the weirdest?

Have a competition to see who can blow the largest bubble. Have the children blow a bubble into the air with their home-made bubble wands or on the table with straws. Using string and a ruler, measure each child's bubble. If you wet the string, you can put it right through a bubble without breaking it. It is a good idea to have small gifts for the winner or winners, such as store-bought bubble wands in the shapes of fish or dinos. For fun you can also give each child a plastic cup filled with Bubble Brew. Have them blow bubbles through a straw into the cup. (Be sure to caution them not to suck the solution into their mouths.)

6. Bubble Prints

Have you ever heard of painting with bubbles instead of a brush? How do you think we can do this? There was an artist named Andy Warhol who was famous for what's known as "pop art." Do you think he did this with bubbles?

This is a great craft activity that gives the children something nice to take home and remember the party by. If you are doing this activity outdoors, be sure the kids are wearing old clothes in case a paint bubble goes astray.

Have three bowls of Bubble Brew on a table. Pour into each bowl 3 heaping tablespoons (15 ml) of powdered tempera paint, one color per bowl, and stir. Now you have three different colors of paint for the children to use.

Divide the children into three groups, and give each child a sheet of paper. Let each group take a turn at each bowl. (A couple of helpers would help save time.) Using a straw, slowly blow a bubble of the first color. Have the first child slip his or her paper under the bubble. Pop the bubble on top of the paper (most bubbles will pop on their own). The paint will fall onto the paper and make a great pattern. Do this with each color for each child, and at the end the children will have great bubble prints.

7. Bubbles That Aren't Round!

Have you ever seen a square bubble? How about a bubble in the shape of a triangle? Let's try to make one.

This is a great experiment to see if bubbles can be blown in different shapes. You may want to create examples of these blowers ahead of time, so that the children can use them as a guide to make their own.

Make a square-shaped bubble blower using two straws and a piece of string about four times as long as one straw. Put the string through both straws, then tie the string together. Now grab a straw with each hand and pull the straws and string into a square.

Next, make a triangular bubble blower using straws and paper clips. You will need three sections of straw about 4 inches (10 cm) long and six paper clips. Clip two paper clips together and stick each free end into the end of a section of straw. Continue to do this until you have made a triangle.

Now try creating a cube shape using straws and string. You will need 12 pieces of straw to do this. Draw a piece of string through four pieces of straw, fold them into a square, then tie the string. Do this again with another four pieces of straw, so that you now have two squares that are the same size. Using four sections of straw, connect the two squares with string or paper clips to make a cube.

Have the children try blowing bubbles with all the different blowers. Can a square blower make a square bubble?

Quick Way: Square, triangular and other premade shaped bubble makers are available at specialty science stores for about $1.50 apiece. You may wish to purchase these ahead of time.

8. Time After Time

You can all blow great bubbles, but whose do you think will last the longest? How long do you think you can make a bubble last?

Get each child to blow a bubble on the table. Using the second hand on your watch, time whose bubble lasts the longest. Have a contest for the best time out of three tries. If you wish, you can get the children to create their own bubble solution and see if the new mixtures give longer-lasting bubbles.

> BUBBLES TO GO: If you have some spare lidded glass jars, you can send home a strange gift. Wet the inside of a jar with water, then add a thick solution of glycerin, syrup, dishwashing liquid, and a small amount of water. Give one prepared jar to each child, and have him or her blow a large bubble with the solution. Cap off the jar and let the child take it home. The bubble inside the jar may last for days!

9. What's Your Angle?

When bubbles touch each other, do they always form the same angles? We can use a tool called a "protractor" to measure the angles that form when bubbles meet. What will the angles be for one, two, or three connected bubbles? What do you think will happen when seven bubbles meet? Will it always be the same angle? Why do you think that is? What might happen when you try to put one bubble on top of another? Let's find out.

Have the children split up into pairs. Ask one child to blow two bubbles on a table that are joined together. Measure the angles that form with a wet protractor.

Pour some Bubble Brew into a glass and have the children dip their straws into the solution and blow. How do the bubbles connect? How many sides do the bubbles have?

> DID YOU KNOW?
> Scientists have been studying bubbles since the fifteenth century. Leonardo da Vinci was not only famous for painting the *Mona Lisa*, but he also investigated liquids too!

10. Caterpillar Bubbles

Let's see if we can create a GIANT bubble bug.

Ask the children to line up along a long plastic table (or a table covered with a plastic tablecloth) that has been soaped with Bubble Brew. Have each child use a straw to blow a bubble as in experiment 2. Have the children try to join their bubbles to create a multibubbled creature.

11. Big, Big Bubbles (optional)

We've made a bubble inside a bubble. How about making a child inside a bubble?

This experiment is best performed outdoors in warm weather. Partly fill an old toddler-type wading pool with Bubble Brew. Attach two plastic ties to opposite sides of a hula hoop (four ties in all), then place the hoop in the pool. Have a child stand with a helper next to the pool with arms by his or her sides. Lift the bubble hoop over the child's head, then pull the hoop down to create a bubble tube.

While the other children are waiting their turn, have them rub an inflated balloon on their hair to create a static charge. Blow a bubble into the air and move the bubble by placing the balloon close to it.

It's a
_____
party!

for:_____

date:_____

time:_____

place:_____

please bring: _____

R.S.V.P.

_____

Lemon Aide

For these experiments you will need a lot of lemons! Look out for a lemon sale at the grocery store or ask your grocer to save "old" ones for you. This is an inexpensive party that is both fun and educational.

Ages: 6 and up

Time: approximately 1 hour

MATERIALS

- ▲ lemons and oranges
- ▲ small bowls or wide cups (one per child)
- ▲ tarnished pennies (about 15 per child)
- ▲ salt
- ▲ steel nails (one per child)
- ▲ steel wool pads
- ▲ soap
- ▲ water glasses
- ▲ confectioners' (icing) sugar
- ▲ baking soda
- ▲ electrical wire
- ▲ wire cutters
- ▲ paper towels
- ▲ aluminum foil (or nickels or dimes)
- ▲ brass thumbtacks
- ▲ steel paper clips
- ▲ flashlight bulbs (one per child)
- ▲ electrical tape
- ▲ bottle
- ▲ balloons

THINGS TO DO BEFORE THE PARTY

- ▲ Two weeks before the party, send out the invitations and begin to gather the materials.
- ▲ Several days before the party, read the instructions and buy the lemons. Make sure you have all the materials.
- ▲ The day of the party, set out the materials and squeeze the juice from about ten lemons. If you wish, you could also use store-bought juice, such as the type found in plastic lemon-shaped bottles. You will still need real lemons for some of the experiments.

PARTY TIME

Although we will be experimenting with lemons, which are normally not harmful, it is important that you do not eat or taste anything unless I tell you that it is okay.

Lemons can be used for many things. Who can tell me what lemons are good for? [Lemonade, pies, flavoring in foods, etc.] *Lemons can also be used to perform interesting experiments.*

1. Put in Your Two Cents' Worth

Did you know that lemons have special powers? Let's investigate some of the things they can do. Does anyone have any clean pennies? How about dirty ones? In case you didn't bring any, I just happen to have some on me that are really dirty. How do you think we can clean them?.

Give each child about 15 tarnished pennies. Then give each child a container such as a small bowl or wide cup. Have each child add about 10 tablespoons (150 ml) of lemon juice to his or her container. Then ask the children to drop the pennies into their containers and swirl them around. Have each child add about ¼ teaspoon (1 ml) of salt to the lemon juice.

Have each child clean a steel nail, using a steel wool pad, soap, and water. Drop the clean nails into the containers with the pennies and leave them untouched for about ten minutes, while you go on to the next experiment. Later, when they check the containers, the children will be surprised to see that the pennies are clean and that the nail has changed to a copper color.

> The lemon juice is an acid. The acid will strip a layer of copper off the pennies. This copper will then react with the acid to cover the nail. This is called "copper plating."

2. Fuzzy Navel

While we're waiting to see what happens to the pennies and nails, let's make ourselves a drink.

Let the children decide between a lemon or orange drink. Have each child squeeze enough juice from the fruit to fill about half a glass. Let the child add about ½ cup (125 ml) of cold water to the fruit juice, and then add about 2 teaspoons (10 ml) of confectioners' or other fine sugar to the glass and stir. Then have them add a heaping teaspoon (about 5 ml) of baking soda (bicarbonate) to the glass and stir. How does it taste?

(By now you can take a look at the coated nail and clean pennies from the first experiment.)

3. Tongue Ticklers

If the last experiment didn't make your tongue tickle, the next one really will. Don't worry. It's not dangerous. It will feel like a tingle!

You will need four pennies per child for this experiment. For each child, cut two 4-inch (10 cm) pieces of electrical wire. With wire cutters, cut off about ½ inch (1.25 cm) of the insulation from each end of both pieces of wire to expose the wire. Give each child a large paper towel and a strip of aluminum foil. Have the children cut four squares each of the paper towel and aluminum foil, slightly larger than a penny. (If you prefer, you can substitute nickels or dimes for the foil.) Ask them to wet the paper towel squares in lemon juice. Tape one end of the first wire to a penny and set this wire aside. Tape one end of the second wire to a piece of aluminum foil (or a nickel), and lay this end on the table. Arrange the pieces of paper towel and foil and the pennies one on top of the other as follows: on top of the taped end of the second wire, towel, penny, aluminum, towel, penny, aluminum, towel, penny, aluminum, and towel. Place the penny end of the first wire on top of the stack, then have the child place the free ends of both wires on the tip of his or her tongue. Shocking!

Do you know what you just made? It is called a "wet cell." Batteries that you use in your radios or hand-held video games are called "dry cells." In the next experiment we're going to make another type of battery. To be safe, you should never put your tongue on any store-bought battery. You could get a bad burn.

4. An Everlemon Battery

Batteries produce electricity. Most batteries contain strong chemicals, which make the battery dangerous if they are broken open, so you should never play with them. What you can do, though, is create your own minibattery with a lemon!

Each child will need half a lemon, the two pieces of electrical wire from the previous experiment, a brass thumbtack, a steel paper clip (not plastic), and a small bulb—like the type you would find inside a flashlight (about 1.5 volts). The paper clip and thumbtack must be of dissimilar metals to function as electrodes. Have each child wrap one end of the first wire around the thumbtack and the other end around the metal tip of the light bulb. The wire must touch the metal tip. If the children have trouble making the wire stick, have them tape it to the metal tip with electrical tape. Ask each child to wrap one end of the second wire around the paper clip and the other end around the screw base of the bulb. Next, have each child push one end of the paper clip into the left-hand side of his or her lemon half. On the right-hand side of the lemon, have the child insert the pointed end of the thumbtack. The light will turn on! This makes a great take-home gift for the end of the party. Try this ahead of time to make sure everything works.

As you have seen in the last two experiments, electricity can be created with an acid and two different metals. This was first discovered by a man named Volta. That's why we now measure electricity in volts.

5. Lemon Blast-Off

Here's a fun, quick experiment. You'll need a bottle, some lemon juice, a balloon, and some baking soda. Place about a tablespoon (15 ml) of lemon juice in the bottle. Put an equal amount of baking soda in the balloon. Cap the bottle off with the balloon without letting any of the baking soda fall into the bottle. When you are ready for lift off, pick up the end of the balloon so that all of the baking soda falls into the bottle. Watch as the balloon inflates and then flies off the bottle.

This is a variation on the volcano experiment from the "Mad Scientists" party. The baking soda and lemon juice react to form carbon dioxide, a gas that inflates the balloon and forces it off the bottle.

6. Lemon Ink

Depending on how much time you have left, you might want to do the "Invisible Ink" experiment on page 25 of the "I Spy" party. This will take about ten minutes. Some of the above experiments take longer to complete, depending on the age of the children.

Lemon Aide

It's a
_____
party!

for:_____

date:_____

time:_____

place:_____

please bring:_____

R.S.V.P.

_____

Watts Up, Doc?

Most children get "wired" at parties, so why not let them get really wired? Children are fascinated by these simple experiments with magnets and electricity. They are always impressed when they themselves create the circuitry that lights a tiny bulb, or when they pick up metallic objects with their own electromagnet. It will also give them a basic understanding of magnetism and electricity.

Ages: 7 to 12

Time: approximately 1 to 1½ hours

MATERIALS

▲ iron filings (available at many toy and hobby stores) (*WARNING:* Be careful when handling iron filings, and don't let the children touch them. The filings can get on their hands and in their eyes.)

▲ glass jar

▲ string

▲ magnets

▲ glycerin

▲ white corn syrup

▲ sheet of clear plastic

▲ Popsicle sticks

▲ plate or container

▲ thick plastic bags

▲ scissors

▲ metal paper clips

▲ ballpoint pens or other pens that will write on plastic

▲ chopsticks or small straight sticks

▲ nonmetallic pan

▲ food coloring

▲ iron nails

▲ C or D batteries (one per child)

▲ electrical wire

▲ wire cutters

▲ electrical tape

▲ small metallic objects (paper clips, thumbtacks, pins, etc.)

▲ 1.5-volt light bulbs (one per child)

THINGS TO DO BEFORE THE PARTY

▲ Scrounge around the house for the materials you need.

▲ See if you can pick up new, inexpensive batteries or, preferably, borrow rechargeable batteries from friends or relatives. Mark the batteries, so you know who to return them to. Carefully examine the batteries to ensure they are in proper working condition and that they have no cracks, seepage, or rust spots. Do not use any batteries that seem "worn." Dispose of batteries in an environmentally sensitive manner. (Contact your municipal government for information.)

▲ Two weeks before the party, send out the invitations and gather the rest of the materials.

▲ The day before the party, read the instructions and make sure the batteries are charged and you have enough for everyone.

▲ The day of the party, set out the materials.

PARTY TIME

Today we're going to do something shocking. We're going to experiment with electricity. And to make this party more—ahem—attractive, we will also be doing experiments with magnets. Some of the things we are working with can be dangerous. Make sure that you don't touch the iron filings with your bare hands, and don't rub your eyes if you have been working with the filings.

1. Iron This Out

These are iron filings, little bits of iron that you can use for some neat experiments. You shouldn't touch them with your bare hands, so we're going to move them around in other ways.

A. Fill a glass jar with water and add a spoonful of filings. Have each child attach a bar magnet to a piece of string. Then let each child take a turn dipping his or her magnet into the solution and slowly drawing it out. Watch the filings move through the water and become attached to the magnet. You may also try to attract filings by placing the magnet on the outside of the glass.

B. Fill a small jar with glycerin and a small amount of iron filings. Dip the bar magnet in as in part A of the experiment. Does the thickness of the liquid make a difference to the power of attraction?

C. Try this experiment with a solution of white corn syrup and filings. Pour several tablespoons (about 25 ml) of this solution onto a sheet of clear plastic (the kind used for covers on book reports—available at most photography or department stores). Move the magnet around below the sheet of plastic to create spikes with the filings. Do not add too many filings, or the solution will be too thick to move.

To clean the filings from the magnets between experiments, use wooden Popsicle sticks. Make sure the children do not touch the filings with their hands, as the filings may get on their skin or in their eyes. Scrape the filings onto a plate or into a container so that they can be reused for the other experiments.

NOTE: Coarsely ground iron filings that resemble grains of sand may be purchased through museums or from manufacturers. Place a magnet over filings to create spikes.

2. Gone Fishing

This is a good activity for the younger kids. You might want to try your hand at fish puns when you introduce the game. For example: "Here's a game for the halibut. I promise it won't make you eel. Don't flounder, or you'll be left behind. We're going to have a whale of a time. Something's fishy if you don't like this activity."

Let the children cut 11 fish shapes from thick plastic bags. Have them attach a metal paper clip to each fish and number the fish from 1 to 10. Number one of the fish -1. Let each child make a fishing pole by tying a chopstick or a small straight stick to one end of a piece of string and a small magnet to the other end of the string. In a nonmetallic pan, mix water and food coloring. Place the fish in the pan and let the children fish for five to ten minutes. Keep track of their scores by marking down the value of the fish caught, then throwing the fish back into the water.

3. Electromagnets

Do you think that a nail can be a magnet? How can we make this nail more "attractive?"

Give each child a nail and let him or her try to attract metallic items with the nail. Ask them how a nail can be changed so that it picks up these things.

Give each child a new C or D battery, one section of electrical wire that is approximately 8 inches (20 cm) long, and an iron nail. Cut off the insulation from both ends of the wire to expose about ½ inch (1.25 cm) of the wire. Have the children wind the wire tightly around the nail, leaving a few inches (about 10 cm) of wire free at each end of the nail so that the ends of the wire can be taped to the battery terminals with electrical tape. When the wire has been attached to both ends of the battery, it forms a circuit. The children will have created an electromagnet that will magnetize the nail, allowing the children to pick up small metallic objects with the nail, such as paper clips, thumb-tacks, pins, etc.

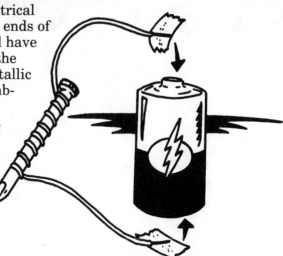

What we created with the batteries and wires is called a "circuit." A circuit is a one-way path that lets electricity travel from one end of a battery to another. If there is a gap or break along the pathway, the electricity will stop flowing because the circuit is incomplete.

4. Turn Me On

Have you ever wondered why a light goes on when you flick a switch? A switch is what opens and closes a circuit like the one we created in the last experiment. Here's how a circuit can light up a bulb.

Use the same setup as in experiment 5. Cut off the wires holding the nail, leaving the two ends of the wire coming off the battery. The two pieces of wire should be about the same length. Attach one wire to a 1.5-volt light bulb (available at hobby or electronics stores). Attach the other wire to the light bulb to complete the circuit.

It's a
_____
party!

for:_____
date:_____
time:_____
place:_____
please bring:_____

R.S.V.P.

_____

Eat Your Experiments

Most kitchens are equipped with all the ingredients of a great chemistry set. If you look through a selection of children's science books, you will find that most recommended materials can be commonly found right in your home. Having kids use these materials to perform their science experiments is not only less expensive, but also safer.

Ages: 5 to 12

Time: approximately 1 to 1½ hours

MATERIALS

- ▲ four bowls
- ▲ apples
- ▲ potatoes
- ▲ radishes
- ▲ onions
- ▲ aluminum foil
- ▲ masking tape
- ▲ marker
- ▲ blindfold
- ▲ *optional:* nose clips
- ▲ disposable cups
- ▲ ice water
- ▲ peanut butter
- ▲ vanilla extract
- ▲ two large glasses
- ▲ aluminum foil or paper
- ▲ ice cubes
- ▲ cola and colorless flavored soft drinks
- ▲ straws
- ▲ watermelon, honeydew, or other melon
- ▲ toothpicks
- ▲ two plates
- ▲ salt
- ▲ wintergreen Life Savers®
- ▲ sweet (unsalted) butter
- ▲ jars with lids (one per child)
- ▲ whipping cream
- ▲ unpopped popcorn, raisins, and shelled peanuts
- ▲ juice glasses
- ▲ soda water
- ▲ citric acid crystals (available at drug stores)
- ▲ baking soda
- ▲ confectioners' (icing) sugar
- ▲ bowl
- ▲ hot dogs
- ▲ flour
- ▲ small hammer
- ▲ *optional:* almond slivers, food coloring, sugar, wooden spoon, and cookie sheet

THINGS TO DO BEFORE THE PARTY

- ▲ Two weeks before the party, send out the invitations and begin to gather the materials. Ask the parents of the guests if any of the children have food allergies or dietary restrictions. Make note if there are.
- ▲ The day before the party, read the instructions and make sure that you have all the materials.
- ▲ The day of the party, set out the materials and prepare the foods that are used in the experiments (i.e., chop the onions, etc.).

PARTY TIME

When you think of food, you don't generally think of science. Nobody wants to put chemicals in their food. Would you put sodium chloride on your popcorn? But what if I told you that sodium chloride is just a fancy name for salt? Have you ever read the contents on the side of a food container or box? [Take several different containers and boxes, such as cereal, canned soups, bottled catsup or cherries, and ice cream, and read the additives to the children.] *Why do you think these products have all these different things inside them? What do you think would happen if they didn't?*

Even if you don't want chemicals in your food, you can still do some fun experiments with them. Some of these experiments have to do with your sense of taste and how it works, and some have to do with foods that have chemical reactions.

If you are serving food at this party, you might want to have some fun with it. You can special-order colored bread from your local bakery, or you can make your own using food coloring and your own or frozen bread dough. Make scrambled eggs colored with blue or green food coloring. Put celery in water with food coloring for several hours, then slice it diagonally. Make purple ice cubes by adding food coloring to the water. How about using white chocolate colored orange or red for the cake? Milk, mashed potatoes, or any other white or light-colored food can also be transformed into a strange and wonderful treat.

If you have several adult helpers, divide the children into small groups and set up the materials for each activity at specific stations. Provide a sheet of instructions for each station. Or one adult helper can supervise each group as he or she goes from station to station and help the children if they get stuck.

1. Food Wars

Everybody here knows what an apple tastes like. Right? Let's see who can taste the apple.

59

Have ready four bowls containing finely chopped or grated apples, potatoes, radishes, and onions (one food in each bowl). Cover the bowls with foil so that the children cannot see what is inside. Use masking tape and a marker to label the bowls "A," "B," "C," and "D."

Blindfold each child and by turn place a nose clip (like the ones you wear when you are swimming) on the child. If you don't have nose clips, simply have the children pinch their noses during the experiment. Have the child stick out his or her tongue and place a tiny amount of one of the items on the tongue. Ask the child if this is an apple. The children can swallow the samples or you can give them disposable cups to spit the sample out. Have the children sip ice water between each taste test. Because their noses can't tell them otherwise, the children will probably say each sample is an apple.

Try the experiment again, this time blindfolding the child and placing either peanut butter or vanilla extract on the child's upper lip. (Don't use the nose clip.) Any difference? Try this experiment with all the children. The smell of the peanut butter or vanilla extract will mask the taste of any other foods.

2. Uh-Huh

Who likes cola drinks and who likes clear pop? Who thinks they can tell the difference?

Wrap two large glasses in aluminum foil or paper so that the children cannot tell what is inside. Fill the glasses with ice cubes. Add cola to one of the glasses and colorless flavored soft drink to the other. Blindfold each child and have him or her take a sip through a straw from each glass. Change straws for each child.

Soft drinks taste very similar. Some of the children may be able to tell the difference, and some will not be able to tell the difference between the two drinks.

3. You Sweet Thing

I need your help to decide which melon is sweeter.

Cut a watermelon, honeydew melon, or any other sweet melon in half. Scoop out the seeds, then peel and cut the melon into cubes, placing toothpicks in each one. Divide the melon pieces between two plates. Lightly salt the melons on one of the plates. Have the children taste the melons from each plate and vote on which one tastes sweeter. Keep a record of the votes. The children wil probably vote unanimously that the salted melon tasted sweeter. Salt enhances the flavor of any food, making sweet foods taste sweeter.

4. Where's the Thunder?

This is a really bizarre experiment and guaranteed to get a laugh. Take a small group of children (three or four) into a room that can be completely darkened. (If the children are young, they may wish to be accompanied by their parent.) If you wish, the children can form a circle facing each other and hold hands. Ask the children if they think that they can create sparks in their mouths. Give each child a wintergreen Life Saver®. Turn off the lights, then tell the children to chomp on the candies with their mouths open while looking inside each other's mouths. The children will see little "flashes" inside each other's mouths. This occurs because friction from chewing the candy creates light which the oil makes visible.

5. Butter Me Up

Have you ever noticed that nearly all commercial butters are the same color? Have you ever wondered why? Many companies add a coloring to the butter so that every batch is always the same color. Let's try making our own butter and compare its color to store-bought butter. Does the color make any difference to the way butter tastes?

Place a stick of unsalted butter on a plate and ask the children if they know how butter is made. Give each child a jar with a tight-fitting lid and pour some fresh whipping cream into each jar. Close the jars and have the children shake the jars until butter forms. Shake for about three minutes. You will know the butter is done when the mixture inside the jar is stiffer than whipped cream. Throw away any liquid left in the jar and taste the butter. Does it taste any different from the store-bought butter? Is the color different?

6. Soda Elevator

Place unpopped popcorn, raisins, and shelled peanuts on the table and ask the children how they can get these items to move without touching or blowing on them. Give each child a juice glass and fill each glass with soda water or other fizzy drinks. Let the kids add several of each item to the glass and watch for a while. Ask them if they can explain what is happening.

The bubbles in the carbonated drink will collect on the items in the glass and eventually cause them to float to the top. When the bubbles break, the items will sink. When more bubbles surround them again, the items will rise to the surface again.

7. Eat a Volcano

You wouldn't want to taste vinegar and baking soda mixed together [the ingredients of the classic "volcanoes" experiment on page 11 of the "Mad Scientists" party]. *Here's an experiment that will make a volcano in your mouth, but it will taste great.*

Help the children mix up 2 tablespoons (30 ml) of citric acid crystals (get these at a drug store), 1 tablespoon (15 ml) of baking soda, and about 9 tablespoons (135 ml) of confectioners' sugar in a bowl. Stir these items well, so that they are thoroughly combined. Give each child a straw and have him or her pick up some of the powder in the straw. Next have the children place the mixture from their straws on their tongues. When the powder comes in contact with their saliva, the chemicals will react and fizz.

8. Adobe Dogs

Have the kids wrap hot dogs (or tofu dogs) in aluminum foil. Make sure there are no openings in the foil. Make clay by mixing about 6 cups (1.5 liters) of flour, 1½ cups (400 ml) of salt, and about 3 cups (750 ml) of water and processing or kneading until smooth. Allow the children to cover the wrapped hot dogs with the clay, using additional clay to create creatures or objects. Bake these in the oven at 350° for about an hour, or until the clay hardens. Gently break the clay open with a small hammer. (Have cooked hot dogs on hand in case all the sculptures do not cook at the same rate.)

Instead of the traditional candle for a birthday cake, how about a nutty candle? Push slivers of almonds into the cake so that the long ends point upward, and light the almonds. The oils in the nut will burn.

You can also make colored "glass" for the kids to take home. Add a few drops of food coloring to sugar and cook the sugar over medium heat, stirring with a wooden spoon. When the sugar has melted into a liquid, pour it onto a greased cookie sheet and allow it to cool. This mixture is extremely hot, so keep children away from it (and be careful yourself!). When the sugar cools, you can break it into pieces.

For a take-home idea, how about candy or frozen treats that "pop"? Several brands are available that make sounds when chewed.

It's a
_____
party!

for:_____
date:_____
time:_____
place:_____
please bring:_____

R.S.V.P.

_____

It's Magic

To most children, science is magic. While there are logical explanations for why a liquid changes color, it still seems like magic to kids. These experiments aren't the usual hocus-pocus variety, but they will still wow the children.

Ages: 6 to 12

Time: approximately 1 hour

MATERIALS

- ▲ salt
- ▲ pepper
- ▲ plate
- ▲ comb or plastic pen
- ▲ old wool sweater or scarf
- ▲ small lidded jars
- ▲ vegetable oil
- ▲ sand
- ▲ iron filings
- ▲ magnet
- ▲ plastic freezer bags
- ▲ transparent tape
- ▲ knitting needle or skewer
- ▲ *optional:* sharpened pencil and produce bags
- ▲ vinegar
- ▲ pennies (two per child)
- ▲ iron nails
- ▲ steel wool
- ▲ empty mayonnaise jar
- ▲ iodine
- ▲ laundry starch (one lump per child)
- ▲ corn syrup
- ▲ glycerine
- ▲ water
- ▲ olive oil
- ▲ rubbing alcohol
- ▲ food coloring
- ▲ containers for colored corn syrup, glycerin, water, olive oil, and rubbing alcohol
- ▲ water glass
- ▲ two saucepans
- ▲ gelatin (two envelopes per child)
- ▲ coffee jar lids (two per child)
- ▲ *optional:* sheets of red and blue plastic
- ▲ white paper
- ▲ green, red, and yellow crayons (one per child)
- ▲ thin cardboard
- ▲ scissors
- ▲ ice pick or other sharp object
- ▲ string
- ▲ pencils or chopsticks
- ▲ candle

THINGS TO DO BEFORE THE PARTY

- ▲ Two weeks before the party, send out the invitations and begin to gather the materials.
- ▲ The day before the party, read the instructions and make sure you understand the experiments.
- ▲ The day of the party, set out the materials.

PARTY TIME

*How many of you have ever seen a magician or a magic show?
Today we're going to be magicians and perform some science
magic.*

1. Mining for Filings

As a preview to the first experiment, perform the "How to Tell
Salt from Pepper" experiment on page 100 of the "Just in Case"
activities. That experiment is a great setup for this trick.

Ask the children if they think the same method will work
with iron filings. Let them try. Now, give each child a small jar
and have them add a mixture of vegetable oil, sand, iron filings
(several tablespoons, about 75 ml, of each), then fill the jar with
water. Tightly close the jar and shake. The filings will float to
the top of the surface while the sand drops to the bottom. Iron
filings stick to the oil which floats on the top of the water. Ask
the children how to remove the filings. Use a magnet to draw
the filings out.

2. Water Balloon

*Have you ever seen a magician stick a needle through a balloon
and the balloon doesn't pop? How about a bag of water?*

A. Working with one child at a time, fill a plastic freezer bag with water, and have the child hold the bag by
the top with one hand and steady the bottom of the
bag with the other. Do not stretch the bag. Place
a piece of transparent tape on the bag, and while
the child is holding the bag of water, take a long
knitting needle or skewer, and in a quick motion
stab the bag where the tape is. You might want to
practice this before the party, and perform this experiment over a basin or outdoors (in case it doesn't work).

B. Try this experiment with a sharpened pencil and a
plastic produce bag (the kind you get at the grocery store).
Blow the bag up and tie it. Poke the pencil through the bag and
see if the bag pops.

The tape is static (doesn't move), so it takes up the surface
tension of the bag, and the bag does not pop.

3. Alchemists

For years people have been searching for a way to turn metal into gold. They haven't found a way to do this yet, but I wonder if there's a way to turn other things into metal?

For each child, fill a small glass jar with vinegar. Have each child add enough salt to just cover the bottom of the jar (not too much), then add two pennies to the jar. Let each child clean a small iron nail with steel wool so that it is shiny. Rinse the nail with water, then drop it into the solution. Let the jars sit undisturbed, while you perform the next experiment.

4. Blackout

This is a wonderful trick for young children. Take a small glass jar (an old mayonnaise jar is perfect) and fill it with water. Without letting anyone see you, add 24 drops of iodine to the water. (Make sure you keep the jar out of reach of the children.) Give each child a small lump of laundry starch (available at most grocery stores). Have the children take turns dropping their lumps into the solution, and watch their expressions! The laundry starch will react with the iodine and turn from white to black. Let the children in on your secret.

> Go back to the nail in the vinegar solution in experiment 3. The nail should be copper colored because the copper from the penny was transferred onto the nail. (You can also do this experiment with lemon juice instead of vinegar. See the "Put in Your Two Cents' Worth" experiment on page 47 of the "Lemon Aide" party.)

5. Amazing Layering

Here's a neat trick to show how liquids of lighter densities float on top of heavier liquids. Because this experiment only works with liquids that don't mix, like water and oil, the layers are made with corn syrup, glycerin, water, olive oil, and rubbing alcohol.

Have all five liquids in separate containers and add food coloring to make each of them a different color. Pour the heaviest liquid, corn syrup, into the bottom of a water glass. Then add the next heaviest, glycerin, by slowly pouring it down the side of the glass, making sure not to mix it with the syrup. Let this layer settle, then carefully add the water, then the olive oil, and finally the rubbing alcohol. You should end up with a glass filled with layers of colored liquids.

6. 3-D Glasses

Here's a bit of magic that makes flat pictures look like they're three-dimensional. They're called 3-D glasses, and here's how to make your own.

Two days before the party, make the lenses. In each of two saucepans over medium heat, for each lens dissolve one envelope of unflavored gelatin in about 3 tablespoons (45 ml) of water and a drop or two of food coloring (one pan with red, the other with blue). Stir the mixtures constantly until the gelatin is dissolved. Remove the mixtures from the heat. Pour the mixtures (keeping red and blue separate) into coffee jar lids or similar containers in ¼-inch (1 cm) layers. You will need enough lids to make one lens of each color for each child. Push the bubbles to the side. Let the gelatin dry for one or two days until it is hard.

The day of the party, lift the hardened gelatin out of the lids—these are now 3-D glasses lenses. Let the children cut the lenses into shapes that are large enough to hold in place over their eyes. If you don't have time to make gelatin lenses, use sheets of red and blue plastic (available at most stationery or photo shops).

Give each child white paper to draw on and green, red, and yellow crayons. Have the children create drawings using these crayons. Try writing secret messages with the green crayon and disguising the message with the red crayon. When viewed through the 3-D glasses, the green should literally jump out. You could also purchase an inexpensive 3-D coloring book (around $2.50) and divide the pages amongst the children.

7. Dancing Snakes

Here's a way to create a toy while doing an experiment.

How do you feel about snakes? Would you like to become a snake charmer?

Have each child draw a coiled snake by making a spiral shape on a piece of thin cardboard. The head of the snake is the outermost point of the spiral, while the tail is the center of the spiral. Have the children cut out the coiled snake shapes with scissors. Using an ice pick or other sharp object, poke a hole through the tail of the snake and tie a string though this hole. Tie the other end of the string to a pencil or chopstick, then hold the snake over a lit candle, making sure that the cardboard is high enough above not to burn.

Amazingly, the snake will start to quickly spin around and around from the heat of the candle.

NOTE: Have water on hand just in case a piece of the cardboard burns.

it's Magic!

It's a
party!

for:_____
date:_____
time:_____
place:_____
please bring:_____

R.S.V.P.

_____

Slime Time

Ages: 4 to 9

Time:
approximately
1 hour

This is an ideal party for younger children who like to get their hands into everything and who like gooey, yucky stuff. It might involve more cleanup than some of the other parties, but it will be worth it to see all the grins.

MATERIALS

▲ measuring cups and spoons
▲ bowls
▲ flour
▲ salt
▲ vegetable oil
▲ pitcher of water
▲ cinnamon
▲ almond or mint extract
▲ food coloring
▲ small bowls or empty margarine containers (one per child)
▲ plastic bags
▲ cornstarch
▲ PVA glue (available at woodworking supply stores)
▲ disposable cup
▲ glycerin
▲ hand lotion
▲ borax
▲ Popsicle sticks or old spoons
▲ *optional:* cake frosting, confectioners' (icing) sugar, and peanut butter

NOTE: It is a good idea to purchase flour, cornstarch, etc. at bulk food stores because it will usually be less expensive than buying it in smaller packages.

THINGS TO DO BEFORE THE PARTY

▲ Two weeks before the party, send out the invitations. Tell the parents to dress the children in play clothes, not "party clothes," as they will be playing with messy things. Begin to look at the experiments and gather the materials.
▲ The day before the party, double-check the materials and do dry runs of some of the experiments you may not be sure of.
▲ The day of the party, set out the materials.

You might consider having separate areas where smaller groups of children can experiment and have fun with all the gooey stuff they will be making. A parent or helper should be at each area to help. If you are doing this birthday party indoors, you need a drop cloth to cover the floors. And don't do the experiments in a carpeted area. A kitchen floor, basement, patio, or even lawn are perfect places.

NOTE: Make sure the children don't eat any of the slime they make.

PARTY TIME

Science is about investigating natural things and creating man-made things. Today we are going to investigate gooey, gukky, slimy things and make some for ourselves.

1. Dough Play

Children love to make and create things with dough. It brings out their artistic and messy side. Dough can be made in any color kids choose, it can be many different consistencies, and it can be molded into any creature or shape. Once a child gets his or her hands on dough, all an adult has to do is let the child play. (But we must warn you, it will be hard for the adult to keep from playing, too!)

At each station, have a measuring cup and spoons; a bowl of flour; a bowl of salt; a bowl of vegetable oil; a pitcher of water; cinnamon; mint or almond extract; and many different colors of food coloring. (*NOTE:* Make sure to check with the grocer about which food colorings cause stains and which do not.)

Each child will need a small bowl or an empty margarine or yogurt container. Have each child add 1 cup (250 ml) of flour and ⅓ cup (80 ml) of salt to his or her bowl and mix. Next have each child stir in 1 tablespoon (15 ml) of oil and approximately ⅓ cup (80 ml) of water and add food coloring to create whatever color the child wants. A pinch of cinnamon or two drops of extract can be added to give a nice smell to the dough. Ask the children to create a space creature, an invention, or their favorite food or toy.

When they are done playing with the dough, they can put the dough in a plastic bag to take home with them or, if they want to save their creations, they can put them aside to dry. Depending on the creation's size, it should be fully hardened within a day.

2. Gooey Gukky

This is an exciting science experiment that is great to play with and feels really neat.

Have a large bowl of cornstarch (approximately two boxes for every ten children), a pitcher of water, a measuring cup, and food coloring. It is best for an adult to mix this and then give some to the children to play with in separate containers. For each cup (250 ml) of cornstarch, add approximately ¼ cup (60 ml) of water. (If the mixture is too dry, continue to add water by the teaspoon until the cornstarch is completely wet but there isn't any water on the surface.) When the mixture is pounded with a fist, it should feel solid; and when held loosely in your hand, it will ooze out. Add a few drops of food coloring to color the mixture.

Cornstarch and water forms what's called a "suspension"—solid particles held together in a liquid. Cornstarch in water is a very special suspension because of the weird way it acts. When you squeeze it in your fist, it feels like a solid; but when you open up your fist, it gets runny like a liquid.

3. Rubbery Putty

Here's a putty you can make that's just like certain store-bought putties. We're going to make a simple plastic that can bend, stretch, and even bounce. It can also take imprints from the news-paper comics.

You'll need to purchase a special glue called PVA (available at specialty or woodworking supply houses). Place about ¼ cup (60 ml) of glue in a disposable cup. Add a drop or two of glycerin, a drop of food coloring, and a tea-spoon (5 ml) of hand lotion and stir. In a separate large container or bowl, add borax to warm water. Keep adding borax until there is about ½ cup (125 ml) of undissolved borax in the bottom of the container. Pour ¼ cup (60 ml) of this supersaturated solu-tion into the glue mixture.

Let the children stir this mixture using a Popsicle stick or old spoon. The mixture will soon begin to look stringy. When this happens, pour in ½ cup (125 ml) more of the borax/water solution and stir. As the plastic begins to form, it will turn into a soft glob that the children can pick up with their hands. Let the children squeeze and play with the glob in the solution until it holds together in the shape of a ball. Let them take the ball out of the solution and play with it. Try bouncing it and using it to pick up the imprint of comics from the newspaper.

If you have time left, here is another quick experiment. Make certain that the children have cleaned their hands very well before doing experiment 4. You can even eat this one!

4. A Sweet End

Put a large container of store-bought (or homemade) cake frosting in a large bowl. Add about 2 cups (500 ml) of confectioners' (icing) sugar and 1 cup (250 ml) of peanut butter. Give each child a blob to knead and model into a take-home goodie.

It's a
_____
party!

for:_____
date:_____
time:_____
place:_____
please bring:_____
R.S.V.P.

_____

Science at Night

12

Ages: 9 to 12

Time: approximately 1 to 1½ hours

Sleep-over parties can be really fun and, despite what you might think, there are many more things you can do at them than watch videos and eat junk food. These experiments will keep the guests busy till it's time to snuggle down, and they'll even get them going the next morning.

MATERIALS

- ▲ milk cartons (two per child)
- ▲ two small mirrors per child
- ▲ masking tape or glue
- ▲ two batteries (C or D)
- ▲ two buzzers or 1.5-volt light bulbs
- ▲ four brass thumbtacks
- ▲ electrical tape
- ▲ two pieces of thick cardboard or wooden slats
- ▲ steel paper clips
- ▲ electrical wire
- ▲ wire cutters
- ▲ *optional:* condenser microphone and earphone
- ▲ cornstarch
- ▲ iodine
- ▲ disposable cups
- ▲ toothpicks
- ▲ cola
- ▲ water glasses
- ▲ pennies
- ▲ milk (not skim milk)
- ▲ food coloring
- ▲ dishwashing liquid

THINGS TO DO BEFORE THE PARTY

▲ Two weeks before the party, send out the invitations asking the parents to have their children bring pillows and sleeping bags or linens. Begin to gather the materials. Save up empty wax-coated, rectangular milk cartons (preferably the 1-quart or -liter size). Make sure you clean and rinse the containers so that there is no milk left inside. Before the party, cut off the tops of the containers, and cut a 3-by-2-inch (7.5-by-5-cm) hole near the bottom on one side of each container (see illustration for experiment 1).

   NOTE: Check out the recipe for disappearing ink in experiment 3. If you are feeling playful, slip in the invitations a note written in disappearing ink to the parents, instructing them not to forget something, such as a sleeping bag. Over the next week or so, the message will disappear, leaving the parents bewildered. If, however, you don't like to play practical jokes, just mix up a batch for the kids to write with.

▲ The day before the party, try out the experiments and make sure you have all the materials. Make sure you have plenty of extra pillows, sleeping bags, and foam pads (if available).

▲ The day of the party, set out the materials.

The trick to a successful sleep-over party is not to invite too many children. The maximum group of kids that any parent can sanely handle is about ten; however, this is a large group to have for a period of 15 hours! Remember, they all have to have somewhere to sleep—either in beds or in sleeping bags.

Start the party, around 7:00 P.M. and have a pickup time around 10:00 A.M. In addition to a large supply of junk food, have a video or two handy for after the experiments. It is customary to tell scary stories just before bedtime. Check out the library for some tales. But be forewarned: If you tell ghost stories, some children may be frightened and not be able to go to sleep. Sleep-overs are recommended for children age 9 and over. A final word of caution: Don't plan a busy day for yourself the day after the party.

PARTY TIME

Rather than the usual kind of sleep-over, we're going to do some science experiments. Some of these experiments won't even be finished until you wake up tomorrow! Let's get started.

1. Periscopes

Have you ever seen old movies about submarines? The captain is always watching the battleships through a periscope. We're going to make periscopes that are great for spying on your brother or sister!

Pass out the milk cartons you have prepared with holes cut in the side, giving two to each child. Have each child place one of the mirrors in the bottom of his or her milk carton, so that the mirror is at a 45-degree angle to the hole, as shown in the illustration. If it helps, fold a piece of cardboard at the correct angle and tape or glue the mirror to the cardboard, then tape the cardboard to the inside of the carton. Have the children do the same thing with the other mirror and carton. Place the open top end of one carton over the open top end of the other carton, so that the two mirrored holes face in opposite directions. Tape the two milk cartons together. Ask the children to practice looking through one of the mirrored holes to see around the corner or over a couch. They can take their periscopes home with them.

2. Calling All Cars!

We're going to work together in teams. Half of you will stay in this room, and half of you will go into another room. We're going to make our own message senders. We'll be able to communicate with each other even though we're in two separate rooms.

Here's a way to get the kids working cooperatively in teams. You will need two adjoining rooms. Have an adult in each room to supervise the construction. Give each team the following: a C or D battery, a 1.5-volt light bulb or buzzer, two brass thumbtacks, electrical tape, a piece of thick cardboard or a soft wooden slat, a steel paper clip (the paper clips and thumbtacks must be of dissimilar metals), and three pieces of wire about 4 inches (10 cm) long with the insulation stripped from the ends of the wires.

Have each team connect one end of the first wire to the negative terminal of the battery and the other end of the wire to the cardboard, using the thumbtack to hold the wire in place on the cardboard. Have them connect one end of the second wire to the buzzer (or light bulb) and the other end to the positive terminal of the battery. They should then connect one end of the third wire to the buzzer (or light bulb) and the other end of the wire to the cardboard with a thumbtack. Make sure the two thumbtacks are close enough that they can be connected by a paper clip (but don't connect them yet).

Bring the teams back together and give them two long wires (long enough to go between the rooms) with the insulation stripped from the ends. Have the teams run the long wires between the rooms. Have one team connect one end of the first long wire to the buzzer (or light bulb) that is connected to the positive terminal of their battery. Have the other team connect the other end of this wire (in the next room) to the buzzer (or light bulb) that is connected to the negative terminal of their battery. Have them do the same with the second long wire, but this time connecting negative to positive. Make sure all connections are correct before you turn on the circuit. Close the circuit of each setup by securing one end of the paper clip to the cardboard with one of the thumbtacks, and then touching the free end of the paper clip to the head of the other thumbtack.

When the circuit is closed, the light or buzzer goes on. This occurs because there is energy flowing freely from one side to the other. If a break occurs in the circuit, the light or buzzer will not work. If this happens, check all the connections to make sure they are secure.

NOTE: Instead of using light bulbs or buzzers, you can make a speaker by using a condenser microphone in place of the paper clip and an earphone in the place of the light bulb. These are available at most electronics stores or can be found in old telephone handsets. If you have an old telephone whose handset unscrews, you can find everything you need in it.

Morse Code

Now we can send each other messages from room to room using Morse code. Morse code, invented by a man named Samuel Morse in 1836, is a system of short (•) and long (—) sounds that are combined in certain ways to stand for letters of the alphabet.

Copy this International Morse Code chart for the children.

a	• —	h	• • • •	o	— — —	v	• • • —
b	— • • •	i	• •	p	• — — •	w	• — —
c	— • — •	j	• — — —	q	— — • —	x	— • • —
d	— • •	k	— • —	r	• — •	y	— • —
e	•	l	• — • •	s	• • •	z	— — • •
f	• • — •	m	— —	t	—		
g	— — •	n	— •	u	• • —		

To send messages, have the children open and close the circuit switch by touching the free end of the paper clip to the thumbtack. To make a "•" make the connection for an instant. To make a "—" hold the connection for a second or so. Send secret messages between the two rooms using Morse code. You can also have the children create their own codes. Make sure that both teams have a copy of the same codes.

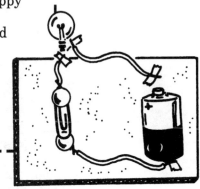

SOME MORSE CODE MESSAGE IDEAS: Send a Happy Birthday message to the birthday boy or girl. Send secrets to the other room. Make up game questions and have the teams signal the answers (have a prize for the team that gets the most correct answers). Tell the children they can also signal each other in Morse code by rapping their knuckles against a hard surface, then see what happens when they all get ready to go to sleep!

3. Disappearing Ink

If the kids haven't had enough of secret messages, give them this "ink" to try. Make the ink yourself, then hand it out in small disposable cups at the party.

Place 1 teaspoon (5ml) of cornstarch in 1 cup (250 ml) of boiling water, and stir until dissolved. Remove any lumps. Add just enough iodine to turn the mixture bluish. Do not be too generous with the iodine, or the recipe won't work. Have the children use this as "ink" with toothpicks to paint or write a message onto paper. This message will disappear over time. Do not taste or drink the ink.

4. A Penny for Your Thoughts

After the guests have been around for a while, you'll probably be left with several half-filled glasses of cola. Combine the cola in one glass so that you have about 1 cup (250 ml). (If you can't recycle, using fresh cola is fine, too.) Have the children drop several pennies into the glass and let this sit overnight somewhere out of reach. *Do not let the children drink it!* In the morning, take the pennies out of the glass. The pennies will be sparkling clean! The phosphoric acid from the cola will have cleaned the pennies.

5. Milking This Experiment

Speaking of leftovers, after breakfast combine leftover milk into a clean glass, or pour some fresh milk (not skim milk) into a saucer. Let the children place a few drops of food coloring into the milk. Do not stir. Dip a toothpick into dishwashing liquid and then into the drops of food coloring.

As soon as the toothpick touches the food coloring, the color will move toward the edges of the saucer. This happens because the detergent in the dishwashing liquid reacts with the fat in the milk. The food coloring helps us to see this occur.

6. Breakfast on the Moon

You've got a bunch of groggy, hungry kids. Make them a colored breakfast, following some of the suggestions for the "Eat Your Experiments" party. Blue milk is always a favorite, as are green eggs. Try writing with food coloring on white bread. Toast lightly for a secret message.

science at **Níght**

It's a
_____
party!

for:_____
date:_____
time:_____
place:_____
please bring:_____

R.S.V.P.

_____

Eggsperiments

Ages: 5 to 10

Time: approximately 1 hour

Eggcellent entertainment can be had all year round, or try this for a terrific Easter party! Have you ever thought that an egg could provide all the makings for great science eggsperiments! You have probably only thought of eggs as food, but as you will see, eggs can be food for thought. So let's get cracking!

MATERIALS

▲ fresh eggs (*NOTE:* freshness is important)
▲ empty mayonnaise jars
▲ salt
▲ glass milk bottles (one for every two children)
▲ bowl
▲ clay
▲ books
▲ *optional:* bathroom scale
▲ candle
▲ wide-mouth glass jar

▲ plastic bag
▲ rolling pin
▲ fireplace matches
▲ white vinegar
▲ kitchen scale
▲ flour or plaster of paris
▲ powdered tempera paints
▲ plastic wrap
▲ wax crayons
▲ small jars

THINGS TO DO BEFORE THE PARTY

▲ Two weeks before the party, send out the invitations and begin to gather the materials. Start saving eggshells. If you don't use many eggs, have your friends, neighbors, or even the parents of the guests save their eggshells. Rinse the shells and remove any raw egg. Gently dry the shells and leave them in a cool place.

▲ The day before the party, read the instructions and make sure that you have all the materials. Prepare the eggs for the various experiments.

▲ The day of the party, set out the materials. Prepare the jars, bottles, bowls, and supplies.

PARTY TIME

What can't you use unless it's broken? The answer to this riddle is eggs. You probably think that eggs are only good for eating, right? Wrong! Eggs are useful for lots of other things. How about Easter egg hunts? Eggs can be used in making shampoo. Today we're going to use eggs to perform some eggciting eggsperiments.

1. Egg Submarines

Let's see if we can get an egg to float. How do you think we can do this?

For every two children, have one empty mayonnaise jar filled with warm water. Have the children measure and add different amounts of salt to the water in their jars and stir well. Place one fresh egg into a jar that contains only water (no salt). It will sink. Have the children add a fresh egg to each of their jars. Depending on the amount of salt added to their jars, the eggs should float at different levels in the jars. Have the children experiment by adding salt, 1 tablespoon (15 ml) at a time, to the water to see how much salt is needed to make the egg float.

2. Good Ship "Egg" in a Bottle

This trick never fails to amaze children of all ages. For every two children, you will need one hard-boiled egg. Have the children carefully peel their eggs, and save the shells (you will need these for other experiments). The peeled egg should just fit into the mouth of a glass milk bottle.

How do you think you can get your egg to fit into your bottle without breaking either the egg or the bottle?

Put the peeled, hard-boiled eggs into a bowl of cold water. Have an adult fill each milk bottle with boiling water and let the bottles sit for a minute or so. Then pour the water out of the bottles into the sink. Let each child immediately place an egg, tapered end down, over the mouth of the bottle. *NOTE: Warn the children not to leave their hands over the top of the bottle or to touch the bottle because it is hot!*

The egg gets sucked inside the bottle because of the difference in air pressure between the outside and the inside of the bottle. The pressure inside the heated bottle is less than the air pressure outside the bottle; therefore, the higher air pressure pushes the egg down into the bottle.

Now that your egg is safely inside your bottle, how are you going to remove it?

Pour any droplets of water out of the bottle. When the bottle is completely dry, have the children turn the bottle upside down, making sure that the tapered end of the egg is facing the mouth of the bottle. Tell each child to lean back and hold the bottle

> *NOTE:* Whenever possible, try to use different puns with the word "egg." You might wish to keep track and offer a prize to the child who most often catches you using puns. For eggzample: eggzactly, eggstra, eggzamine, eggstaordinary, eggcellent, and eggcetera. Don't forget puns using the words "yolk" or "chicken."

above his or her head and blow into the mouth of the bottle (this will need to be tried several times). The children will need great patience, but with practice the egg should pop out of the bottle. If the egg is cracked or in pieces, don't try this experiment.

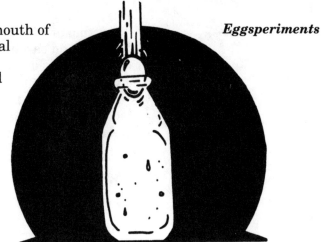

3. What Time Is It When an Elephant Sits on an Egg?

What time is it when an elephant sits on an egg? It's time to get a new egg. Seriously though, an egg's shape makes it very strong. That's why eggs don't break when the hen sits on them.

It is best to perform the first part of this experiment over a bowl, just in case something goes wrong.

A. Put the tapered end of a raw egg between the palms of your hands and squeeze the egg. As long as you started with an uncracked egg, you probably won't have broken the shell.

B. Place the broad ends of four uncooked eggs into clay (to hold them in place) in a rectangular formation. Make sure that the tapered ends of the eggs point upward. Then try this great game to see how many books the four eggs will hold. If you have a bathroom scale handy, you might weigh the books to see how much weight the eggs can handle. Have the children guess how many books the eggs will hold. Carefully place one book on the eggs. Did it hold? Continue to place more books on the eggs till they can't hold any more books.

4. An Eggstinquisher

How do you think a little egg could put out a fire? Watch this.

Place a 3-inch (7.5 cm) high candle in a wide-mouth glass jar (such as an old mayonnaise jar). It is a good idea to melt the bottom of the candle before placing it in the jar so that it will stand upright.

While you are preparing the jar, have the children put the shells from two eggs in a plastic bag, then use a rolling pin to crush the shells into a fine powder. Place the crushed eggshells on the bottom of the jar. Using a fireplace match, light the candle. Quickly and carefully, drizzle about ½ cup (125 ml) of vinegar down the side of the jar onto the eggshells, being careful not to let any vinegar splash onto the flames. Like magic the flame is extinguished.

The chemical reaction between the eggshells and the vinegar created carbon dioxide, a gas that put out the flame.

5. Eggsercising

How do you think you can make an egg move on its own?

Give each child a fresh uncooked egg. Have the child spin the egg quickly on its side for about 30 seconds. Tell the child to stop the egg by gently pressing on it briefly with one finger. The egg should continue to spin slowly. This happens because the fluid inside the egg is still moving.

6. Which Egg Is Which?

How can you tell whether an egg is hard-boiled or raw without breaking it?

Have the children shake, spin, weigh, and observe two eggs— one hard-boiled, the other raw. See if they can come up with the correct answers without breaking the eggs. You can tell two ways: (1) the hard-boiled egg spins faster, and (2) when the eggs are stopped, the raw egg will continue to spin, but the hard-boiled egg won't.

7. Flip-Over Eggs

If you look around some toy stores, you can sometimes find a spinning top that looks like a whole mushroom. When this top is spun, it flips upside down and turns on its stem. Did you know you can do this with a hard-boiled egg?

Have each of the children spin a hard-boiled egg on a wide, flat surface, or let an adult spin the egg. The egg must spin very fast, and the eggshell must not be cracked. As the egg spins on its side, its broad end will begin to rise, and the egg will balance on its tapered end. There is a very complicated explanation for this that is taught in most university physics courses.

8. Egg Chalk

This is a fun take-home gift. It takes the eggshells of approximately two large eggs to make one stick of chalk.

Now that you have all those eggshells, here's a great way to use them and give each child a unique and inexpensive take-home gift. Have the children put clean egg shells into a plastic bag and use a rolling pin to crush the eggshells into a fine powder. Clean away all membrane from the eggshells. Make sure all the shells are finely ground and that there are no big chunks. Add 2 tablespoons (30 ml) of either flour or plaster of paris for every tablespoon (15 ml) of eggshells. For colored chalk, add a small amount of powdered tempera paint. Add enough water to make a paste. Place a 2-by-2-inch (5-by-5-cm) blob of the paste onto a piece of plastic wrap, and roll it into a tubular shape. Tell the children to let the paste harden before they unwrap and use the chalk.

9. Egg Batiks

Does anyone know what batiking is? Batiking is a form of art where the material is covered by colored wax and then dyed. When the wax is ironed and removed, the dye seeps through the cracks in the wax, leaving colored lines in the dyed material. We're going to do this using eggs and crayons.

> *NOTE:* This is an interesting way to color Easter eggs.

Give each child a hard-boiled egg and let him or her color the egg with wax crayons. Tell the child not to cover the entire egg with the crayon. A small simple design is best. Have the child place the egg in a small jar filled with vinegar, and cover the mouth of the jar loosely with plastic wrap.

WARNING: Do not put a tight cover on the jar because the carbon dioxide produced by the reaction between the vinegar and eggshells will put pressure on the jar, possibly causing it to burst.

The children can take their jarred eggs home with them. Instruct each child to remove the egg after about six hours and gently rinse the egg off. The vinegar will have dissolved the eggshell, but the wax from the crayon will have protected the shell. The child will be left with a soft egg and a hard design. (The eggs are not edible art.)

EGGSPERIMENTS

It's a
party!

for:_____
date:_____
time:_____
place:_____
please bring:_____

R.S.V.P.

_____

Eau d'Odor

Kids love to make their own candles, soap, and potpourri. If you are looking for the perfect party for a group of young ladies, or a party for both boys and girls, this may be the one for you. Remember to use old pots, pans, spoons, and utensils, or rid your cupboards of all those old food containers for this party.

Ages: 6 to 12

Time: approximately 1 hour

MATERIALS

- ▲ small plastic or paper containers (such as milk cartons)
- ▲ sand
- ▲ kitchen utensils (such as cookie cutters)
- ▲ wick
- ▲ paraffin
- ▲ old pot
- ▲ crayons or tempera paint
- ▲ mugs (one per child)
- ▲ soap flakes
- ▲ salt
- ▲ wooden spoon
- ▲ food coloring
- ▲ perfume
- ▲ spices
- ▲ bowls
- ▲ dried flowers
- ▲ wood chips
- ▲ orange, lemon, or lime peels
- ▲ squares of material (about 3 × 3 inches, or 7.5 × 7.5 cm) or the foot parts of old stockings
- ▲ ribbon or yarn
- ▲ sheets of beeswax
- ▲ hand soap (unscented, nondeodorant)
- ▲ plastic containers (such as yogurt containers)
- ▲ plastic knives

THINGS TO DO BEFORE THE PARTY

- ▲ Two weeks before the party, send out the invitations and begin to gather the materials.
- ▲ The day before the party, try out the experiments, making sure that you have all the materials.
- ▲ The day of the party, set out the materials.

Have a wet washcloth handy and some paper towels in case of any spills. You may wish to put a drop cloth down or plastic covering on the table, as it may get wet.

PARTY TIME

Today we are going to be scientists, but instead of using man-made chemicals, we are going to use science to create useful things from nature.

1. Sand Castle Candles

How can you make a candle with sand? Let's make some different shaped candles.

Have the children line the inside of small plastic or paper containers, such as milk cartons, with wet sand. The sand should stick together like a snowball. After the sand has coated the inside of the container, the children can create designs in the sand by scraping the sand with different kitchen utensils, such as a butter spreader, or by pressing designs into the sand with cookie cutters.

When the designs are finished, have the children place a wick in the bottom of the container, leaving about 3 inches (7.5 cm) extra hanging out the top of the box. While the children are preparing their boxes, melt paraffin in an old pot over a double boiler or pan. You can add bits of old crayons or tempera paints to color the mixtures. Make several colors using this method. Have the children stand back from their boxes. Carefully pour the *hot* wax into the molds. Allow the wax to cool off till it has set. Warn the children not to touch the wax until you tell them it's okay, as they could burn themselves.

CAUTION: Melted wax is very hot. Close supervision and instruction is necessary when children are handling this material.

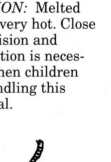

When the wax has hardened, have the children turn the molds upside down. Most of the sand will fall away, and the children will see their sand castle candles. If the children carve or scrape away the sand that clings to the wax, they will have textured candles. You can also try adding ice cubes to the mold before pouring the wax in. This will displace some of the wax, producing a candle that looks as if it has been eaten by moths.

2. Salty Soap

Children are fascinated by this next experiment. You would never expect that it would work.

Soap is something you use every day—at least I hope you use it every day. Have you ever thought about how soap is made? Well, this isn't it! We're going to make some very strange soap.

Give each child a large mug, and fill the mug with ½ cup (125 ml) of hot (but not boiling) water. Let each child add about 3 tablespoons (15 ml) of soap flakes to this water and stir until the flakes have dissolved. In a large pitcher, pour ½ cup (125 ml) of hot tap water for every child (for example, for ten children use 5 cups (1.25 liters) of water). For each ½ cup (125 ml), add 2 heaping tablespoons (10 ml) of salt and stir the mixture with a wooden spoon. Should the children want colored and/or scented soap, add food coloring, perfume, or even spices (such as cinnamon) to the soapy water.

Carefully pour ½ cup (125 ml) of the salt water into each child's mug. *Do not stir!* Allow the soap to float to the top of the mugs (in approximately one minute), then have the children scoop it out and shape it into figures.

For another great soap recipe, check out "No Excuses Soap" in *Projects for a Healthy Planet*, Levine/Grafton, John Wiley & Sons, 1992.

3. Sock-Pourri

Have any of you every heard of something called "potpourri?" Do you think that it is pourri in a pot? Potpourri is correctly pronounced "poe (as in toe)-poor-e," and it is made from dried flowers and spices mixed together to make a room smell nice. Instead of using scented sprays from a can, you can make your own fragrances.

Have small bowls of various naturally fragrant items on the table. Some suggestions are cinnamon; cloves; roses; lilac; sweet peas; carnations; peonies; violets; wood chips; and orange, lemon, or lime peels. Allow each child to put together a mixture of the above, by scooping spoonfuls into a shallow bowl or plate. Give each child a 3-by-3-inch (7.5-by-7.5-cm) square of material, or the foot part of an old stocking, in which to place the mixture.

Tie the bundles of potpourri with colorful ribbon or yarn, and let the children take them home.

4. None of Your Beeswax

You can purchase or order sheets of colored or plain beeswax (available at most hobby and crafts shops). Trim the sheets diagonally, and cut a wick that is about 3 inches (7.5 cm) longer than the beeswax. Have the children roll the sheet around the wick so that the wax will be thickest on the bottom of the candle. These are the nicest smelling candles you can find!

5. Soap Carving

If you are entertaining younger children, you might want to prepare this recipe a few days ahead of the party. For each child, mix 5 tablespoons (75 ml) of chopped hand soap (nondeodorant, unscented type) with 3 tablespoons (45 ml) of water. In an old pot or throwaway pan, cook the mixture over low heat, stirring continually. When the mixture develops a gluey texture, add chopped bits of old crayons, and continue to stir until the crayons melt. Scoop the mixture into old plastic containers, such as yogurt containers. At the party, give each child a slab of this mixture and a plastic knife or other dull instrument with which to carve the soap.

Eau D'Odor

It's a
party!

for: _____

date: _____

time: _____

place: _____

please bring: _____

R.S.V.P.

_____

"Just in Case" Activities

Nothing is foolproof! Sometimes parties finish early. Sometimes parents are late picking up their kids. Sometimes you just need something else to fill up five minutes. If you are in trouble, try some of these lifesavers.

1. Balloon Static

Blow up or have the kids blow up balloons. Have them rub the balloons on their hair or on their clothes to create static electricity. Stick the balloons on the walls, or see who can get their hair to stand up the most. Rip paper into little pieces, and use the charged balloons to pick up the paper. Have the children crumble Styrofoam® packing chips into tiny pieces, then rub balloons over their hair and try to pick up the pieces with their charged hair or the balloons.

2. Hanging Stethoscopes

If you've got a rowdy group of young children, this is a great way to keep them busy. Give each child a wire coat hanger and two pieces of string. Have each child tie the strings to the hanger, one string at each of the bottom corners, then invert the hanger so that the hook part hangs downward. Tell the children to take the free ends of each string in each hand and gently place their fingers, with the string, next to or just at the opening of their ears. (Warn the children not to put the hanger or anything sharp in their ears.) The hanger should fall just below the child's hips. The kids can now walk around the room, banging into objects like chairs, desks, doors, or anything else that is not breakable, and they will hear some amazing sounds. The children can take home their vibration detectors.

3. How to Tell Salt from Pepper

Put equal amounts of salt and finely ground pepper on a plate. Vigorously rub a comb or plastic pen for several minutes on an old wool sweater or scarf. Hold the charged item about 1 inch (2.5 cm) or so above the plate, and watch the pepper jump up. Try this with a charged balloon. Don't hold a charged item too close to the mixture, as the salt will also be attracted.

4. Runaway Pepper

Place enough water on a shallow, rimmed plate to cover the entire surface of the plate. Have the children sprinkle salt and pepper on the water. Have one of the children touch the center of the water with his or her finger. Give the same child a bar of soap and have him or her touch the same spot, this time with the tip of the soap. Watch the expression on the kids' faces as the pepper heads toward the rim of the plate.

5. Ice Fishing

Put an ice cube in a glass of water. Cut a piece of string about 5 inches (13 cm) long. Place the string across the ice, and sprinkle salt over the string and ice. Wait a minute, then lift the ice up by the string.